To:

I0141272

From:

May you feel the peace and share the power of a positive perspective today… and every day.

Gary A. Pokorn

Acknowledgements

To my wife and my life's inspiration, Debbie.

To my friend Steve Whitehead. Without him, this book would have remained only in my imagination.

Gary A. Pokorn

<u>The Peace and Power of a Positive Perspective</u>

by Gary A. Pokorn

Copyright 2010 Registration Number TXu001707771

Cover Designed by Doug Hunley

Table of Contents

How Steve & Gary Made it Home for Christmas

Christmas week and I'm in Baltimore, Maryland. In this post-9/11 world the airlines have been transformed. It used to be you could just show up at the airport and change your ticket to another flight almost at will. Especially for us seasoned, "1 K", road warriors. But in 2006, not so much. Well, I was booked on an evening flight home on Wednesday, December 21st and in over 25 years of business travel; I had never not made it home for the holidays.

Wednesday - I was wrapping up my last business trip of the year. We just finished lunch so I checked messages before going into my last meetings of the day. The first voice mail message was from the airline – a computer generated voice told me my flight home has been cancelled. The second message was from my wife – "it's snowing heavy in Denver" with a little more than just a matter-of-fact tone in her voice. My first call was to neither the airline nor my wife – I called the hotel I had checked out of earlier that morning and reserved a room for tonight; just in case. (Not my first rodeo.) I'd call my wife back later.

My client decided to shorten our afternoon meetings – after all, it was four days before Christmas. They thought maybe I could catch an earlier flight home. I thanked them for their consideration without mentioning the weather conditions in Denver. In the taxi back to the hotel I called my wife. "We're having a blizzard" she blurted, "They've closed the Denver airport" and followed almost crying," Are you going to be able to get home for Christmas?" "Sure Dear", I responded, "Don't worry. You know I've been a road warrior for 20 years. I'll make it home just fine." I listened to see if she heard any hint of confidence in my voice while in the back of my mind I was wondering, "How the hell *am* I going to get home for Christmas?"

Permit me to fast-forward through checking back into the hotel; my numerous attempts to call the airline – any airline! In a somewhat move of desperation I even looked into the train and bus schedules from Baltimore, Washington D.C., or New York City to Denver. Finally, after waiting on hold through a room service dinner and two pay-per-view movies, the airline customer service agent eventually came on the line. "Mr. Pokorn, I can confirm you on the first flight in the morning, non-stop to Denver, with an exit row aisle seat, departing from Baltimore on Monday - December 26th." Like I said, "How the hell am I going to get home for Christmas?"

I confess that for just an instant I gave some thought to the idea of enjoying an extended stay at this comfy hotel; eating room service and just relaxing; what I like to call de-compressing. All at the courtesy of my client's expense account. But then I snapped back to reality.

She was still up when I called. By then, the kids had come over to the house with their overnight bags and their dogs; even our good friend Jacque came over.

Her husband, Steve, was also out of town on business and she didn't want to be home alone during a blizzard.

Of course Jacque didn't originally plan on it being a sleep-over. But after her afternoon visit extended into the early evening, two obstacles were going to prevent her from driving back home tonight. First, her car wouldn't start. My younger son, who was an auto mechanic at the time, looked at it and decided the blizzard coupled with the cold temperatures had probably frozen the fuel line. "Let it sit and it will probably thaw out in the morning", was his advice. The second obstacle was Jacque had been drinking wine with my wife as they worried about how Steve and Gary were going to make it home for Christmas. Not good for her to get behind the wheel of a car.

My wife answered the phone with the hopeful question, "Are you at the airport?" "No, by the time I got through to the airline the earliest flight they had was for Monday morning" I replied as matter-of-factly as I could. "Monday?! Next Monday? The Monday after Christmas? You're going to miss Christmas?" She was making her statements in rapid succession and in the form of questions. (Too much Jeopardy.) As calmly as I could I said, "Honey, I've rented a car and I'm just going to drive home." Silence on the other end. "You know, I've done this before" I added. "Remember the time I drove home from Philadelphia right after the 9/11 terror attacks?" Silence. "Well, I'm leaving first thing in the morning. I'll be home by Friday night." And I proceeded to share the details of my game plan with her.

Of course, I know I'm the husband – and she's the wife, so she's naturally wondering in the back of her mind, "He's a man – what does he know?" Nevertheless, I knew my plan was solid, and probably the only chance I had to make it home for Christmas.

It was 698 miles from Baltimore to Chicago – the "Plan A" in my game plan. I knew I could drive that distance in a Yugo if I had to. But I had rented a full-size Oldsmobile; and best of all, it came with satellite radio! "This would be a piece of cake", I said. My wife listened dutifully as I described each element of "Plan A". I would arrive at the rental car counter at Baltimore-Washington International Airport (BWI) tomorrow morning when they open at 6:00 a.m. I'll be on the road and into the Maryland countryside before rush hour. As I drive west on the interstate highway system I'll call the airlines to see if I can catch a flight as I near each major city: Pittsburgh, Cleveland, Columbus, Toledo, Detroit, Indianapolis, Chicago-Midway, or Chicago-O'Hare; all the while, I'm getting closer to home. "I'm sure one of the airlines will have a single, open seat on a flight to Denver" I said as I concluded all of the details of "Plan A". If I hit the Indiana-Illinois border without a flight and the weather starts to turn bad, I'll simply turn north, drive to Chicago and stay with Debbie's Mom. On the other hand, if I get that far and the weather is good, I had a "Plan B". I will drive into eastern Iowa; arriving by 10:00 p.m. or so; and stay the night. If I reach Iowa by Thursday night, the 22nd, it will be a piece of cake getting home for Christmas from there, no matter what

the weather conditions are. That was my game plan –
and I was proud of it.

After again listening dutifully, there was a short
pause to make sure I was through. Then my wife
responded, "You can't drive all the way home from
Baltimore by yourself, it's too far" she stated firmly and
logically the way many wives often do. "We'd be
worried sick and remember the blizzard?" emotion
starting to peek-a-boo into her voice. "As you're driving
west the blizzard will be heading east. It will pick up
moisture from the Gulf of Mexico as it crosses into
Kansas and Nebraska." Now I could hear the fear-
spiked adrenaline starting to flow into her voice as she
was speaking faster and louder. "With nothing but
flatlands in the way, by the time you meet the storm in
Iowa it will have gale-force winds; dumping snow by
the foot; spreading highway wreckage and devastation
of unseen proportions; and THE WORLD AS WE
KNOW IT WILL COME TO AN END!" she shrieked
on 100% emotional octane! But I thought, "She's my
wife – what does she know?" So we agreed to disagree
(which is much easier to do over the phone than in
person) and called it a night. Maybe the airline would
call before the morning to say they had an open seat for
me; maybe even one in first class. Yea! right!

Thursday, December 22nd, 5:45 a.m. Eastern
Standard Time. The car rental counter at BWI opened
early; I have my Oldsmobile; I'm on the highway; I'm
heading west. Cake!

There's not much to say about a 700-mile drive on the interstate highway system from Baltimore towards Chicago. Suffice it to say that the weather was clear and having a 200+ station, satellite radio system was great. My game plan was working out just as I planned until I realized my first oversight. I had a cell phone, but only a wall-charger for it that I used in the hotel. I left my car-charger at home for this trip because I hadn't originally planned on spending 36 hours in a rental car. So, I had a choice. I could get off of the interstate, look for an electronics store and buy a car charger; or not. I decided on the or not. This drive was going to be long enough. I didn't want to add an unplanned shopping excursion. Since I was going to pull over at rest stops every 3 hours or so anyway to stretch my legs and refill my coffee, I figured I would just plug into a wall outlet at each rest stop and call home. In between stops, I could make a quick call if I had to on a low battery. Of course by now you're probably thinking, "He's a consultant – what does he know?"

When I made my first rest stop, I shared this modification to my game plan with my wife; I think she was probably agreeing with you. Nonetheless, that's how it worked. My rest stop calls weren't long enough to fully recharge my cell phone, but I was able to check in at home, see if an airline flight had opened up, and pick up a little battery boost, all at the same time. By the time I reached the Pennsylvania-Ohio border, I felt I could even make a few calls while driving without totally draining the battery. See what I mean? Cake.

By now I was realizing that the odds of getting an unreserved seat on a flight to Denver, after a blizzard, and three days before Christmas were zero. So it became obvious that this was going to be a full road trip all the way home. This reality check led me to the second oversight in my game plan as I thought out loud, "I wonder where I'm going to sleep tonight?"

I went over the interstate route in my mind again. I had driven across Pennsylvania on the Turnpike and stayed on Interstate-80/Ohio Turnpike as I crossed the state line. No less than ten heavy metal stations blaring on the satellite radio (not to mention continuous intakes of sugar and caffeine) made getting to this point fairly easy. When I hit Indiana I knew I would transition onto toll-free Interstate 80 and take that straight through into western Nebraska – weather permitting of course. I thought for a moment, "Blizzard? What blizzard?"

I focused back on my original game plan. When I approach Illinois, if the weather was bad, I'll turn onto Interstate 55 and drive an hour north into the Chicago suburbs to stay the night with my Mother-In-Law. I had noticed that none of the 12 satellite radio stations dedicated to weather and road conditions were reporting any winter driving advisories or weather alerts for Indiana or Illinois. All of the weather flashes were about the blizzard that was crippling Denver. So it seemed to me that by tonight I could actually be sleeping in eastern Iowa. But where?

At the next cell-phone-plug-in, rest stop, exit on the Ohio Turnpike I called home. "Everyone here is fine. We're drinking wine and playing cards" was the much more cheerful greeting from my wife. "It's still snowing like hell and now all of the roads are closed" she added as her attention turned away from their cozy slumber party to the fact that I was driving through Ohio and not in my jammies, pouring wine with the family. "Not to worry Dear", I replied in an upbeat tone of voice (probably the effects of the caffeine and sugar in my bloodstream from all of the junk food and coffee I had consumed over the past 460 miles – better check out the country western radio stations for a while). "I won't reach Colorado until tomorrow night and by then they should have all of the roads plowed" I added. I listened to see if she heard any hint of confidence in my voice while in the back of my mind I was thinking, "How the hell are they going to clear the highways by then?" "But that's not why I'm calling" I said, wanting to get back to the task at hand. I asked her to check on weather forecasts for Illinois, Iowa, and Nebraska for the next 12 to 24 hours and also see what hotel options I had for tonight. I thought I could reach the Mississippi River, maybe even drive 10 to 15 miles into Iowa by tonight. Then we hung up, but not before agreeing to rendezvous again in 3 hours and discuss her findings.

Back on the interstate I started to think about other evening accommodation options I might have. "Maybe I could stay with the Lindsay's?" I speculated. But my college fraternity brother Bob and his wife Donna lived in Galesburg. That was 34 miles south of Interstate 80 in western Illinois, which would be a 68-mile diversion –

adding another hour or more to my journey home. My mind then jumped to "What about Steve?" Steve was Jacque's husband; the same Jacque who was drinking wine, playing cards, and enjoying a neighborhood pajama party at my house courtesy of the blizzard. Steve was working on an assignment in eastern Iowa and that might be the perfect overnight stopping point for me tonight. That is, if he's still there and hasn't already left for home. I thought I had enough juice in my cell phone to give him a try.

"Hello", he picked up on the first ring. "Hey Steve, it's Gary Pokorn", and we proceeded through the usual few minutes of small talk, when I got to the main point. "Steve, how are you getting home for Christmas?" After a short pause he said, "You know, I was just thinking about that when you called. In fact, I was hoping this was a call from the airline. My flight out of Midway has been cancelled" noting that he had received a similar phone call from a computer earlier today. "I can't get through to the airlines to see if they've re-booked me on another flight", he added. One of the problems with an airline reservation computer is it will call you but you can't call it. Obviously, this was deja-vu all over again in my mind. "What about you" he asked. "Well, I'm westbound on Interstate 80 passing by Toledo. Want me to pick you up in the morning?" I offered. "You're driving home?" he clarified. "Yes, my flight from Baltimore was cancelled yesterday so I left this morning, early." And we proceeded through the usual few minutes of small talk slamming the airlines.

"Well, I have a rental car that has to be returned to Midway" Steve said, returning our attention back to the task at hand. "Can't you just drop it off in the Quad Cities?" I suggested. "Maybe, but there would probably be an extra drop-off fee" Steve replied, sort of thinking out loud. Knowing my cell phone battery was only a few amps away from dying, I wanted to wrap up this call. "I'll tell you what. You check it out and I'll call you back when I'm in Indiana. We can either hook up in Chicago or in the Quad Cities if you want to hitch a ride with me." "OK" Steve replied, "But don't count on me. I may just get another flight out of Midway."

Rather than pulling off of the highway, I chanced one more call home to update my wife. When she answered the phone I prefaced our conversation with the need to keep the call very, very short because of my dwindling phone battery. She must have been sitting near Jacque because when I told her about my discussion with Steve I could hear Jacque asking what was going on. When I related Steve's reluctance to drop his rental car off at the Quad Cities airport in Moline, Illinois because of the extra fee, Jacque took the phone from my wife. "Gary? It's Jacque. I'll call Steve and see what he's thinking" she stated with definite purpose in her voice. In the back of my mind I was thinking what she really meant was, "Steve's my husband – what does he know?" And we agreed that I would call back when I reached central Indiana to see what she and Steve decided.

By now you might have noticed the communications problem we were having. Since my cell phone could only be used for short, one-minute calls in between rest stops, plug-ins every three to four hours, trying to coordinate things among Debbie, Steve, Jacque, the airlines, a hotel, and weather updates was a joke. Of course, at Debbie and Jacque's end the blizzard conditions periodically interrupted the humor and fun with a bit of frenzy as they were genuinely worried about how Steve and Gary were going to make it home – <u>safely</u>, never mind for a moment, making it home by Christmas. Also, Steve and I were somewhat on our own to think through this problem; and obviously, we are men – what do we know? Nonetheless, the facts were: I was driving west; Steve was assessing his options; wine was starting to run low at the pajama party; and it was still snowing hard in Denver.

When I was within a couple of hours of the Indiana-Illinois border, I made my next phone-power, rest stop. I called Steve first. By this time he knew he couldn't get another flight out before Christmas – same as me. He was able to confirm that if he dropped his rental car off in Moline vs. Chicago it would cost an additional $300. He said he had talked it over with Jacque and he was leaning towards staying with his Mom in Bettendorf, Iowa; staying with his Sister-In-Law in Dubuque, Iowa; or possibly returning his rental car in Chicago and just taking his chances on catching a stand-by flight to Denver Christmas Eve. "OK by me" I said, "See you in Denver. Travel safe" and we concluded our chat. I knew I was rapidly approaching a point-of-no-return if Steve changed his mind and wanted to meet me in Chicago. I made a mental note to call in one last time before I passed that point.

I then called home for my next signal check with Debbie. "Honey, were you able to find me a hotel room for tonight?" I started. "Yes, you're all set at the Holiday Inn in Iowa City and it's only ½ mile off of I-80" she said proudly. Perfect. I think Iowa City was just 20 or 30 minutes west of the Mississippi River, and the hotel was so close to the interstate that my Plan B was unfolding just like I envisioned. "What about Steve?" she asked. "Well, I think he's going to take a pass on my offer to drive him home. He seems concerned about the cost of returning the rental car" I concluded. I could tell Jacque was again nearby because I could hear her say in the background, "Let me call Steve." So Debbie asked me if I could call back in 30 minutes so Jacque could finalize things with Steve. "OK, but I'll be back on the highway by then with little left in my cell phone battery so we'll have to keep it short" I concluded.

I'm not exactly sure how the next conversation went between Steve and Jacque, but I can imagine. I didn't really know Steve that well at the time but it seemed ironic to me that by this point Debbie and Jacque were telling Steve to drive home with me. After all, it was just last night that I was the crazy-man in my wife's eyes for coming up with the idea of a road trip from Baltimore home. Now they were thinking Steve was the crazy-man because of his concern over a rental car drop-off fee. I suppose in the eyes of our kids they were thinking we were all crazy, adding – "They are our parents; what did they know?"

When I called back home 30 minutes later, my wife quickly stated, "Call Steve. He's coming home with you. Bye." Definitely a battery-conserving call. My conversation with Steve was short, too. "Yea Gary, Jacque thinks I should come with you so let's meet at the Quad Cities Airport tomorrow morning at 6:00 a.m., OK?" "See you in the morning", I replied, "and I'll have a fully charged cell phone by then so call me anytime after 5:00 a.m. if you need to." And Plan B was now in full force.

It was well after dark when I reached the Indiana-Illinois border. The roads were still clear and it wasn't snowing, but it was very foggy for some reason known only to the weather gods. So my drive across Illinois was a bit slower than I preferred, but I reached Iowa City a little after 10:30 p.m. The hotel's restaurant was still open, so I ate first and checked in second. A hot shower and a comfortable bed capped off a perfect Day One of my road trip. I counted my blessings before falling off to sleep.

In the morning I left early because I needed to back track about fifty miles to hook-up with Steve at the airport in Moline. That's Moline, Illinois – yes, I was back on the east side of the Mississippi River again. At least it wasn't snowing (yet).

Steve and I met up at the Avis counter at 6:00 a.m. just like we planned. Unfortunately, unlike Baltimore yesterday, the folks in Moline were running late. However, by 7:00 a.m. Steve had returned his car, paid the extra $300 drop-off charge (Merry Christmas Avis), and bought our first cups of coffee-to-go. We were on our way. It was Friday, December 23rd and with luck, we would be home tonight with time to spare to enjoy the holidays. Cake.

Steve and I were casual friends, having originally met through our wives' wine group friendship. Of course a 16-hour road trip was going to make our friendship all the better. I bet you can guess the sequence of our topics of conversation as we returned to Interstate 80. First, it was the blankety-blank car rental company; then the blankety-blank weather; then the blankety-blank airlines; and finally the blankety-blank Broncos. We are from Denver after all, and since John Elway's retirement our Broncos have not been very impressive. By the time we passed Des Moines, Iowa the early morning fog had cleared and we had just about run out of small talk. We did get a big chuckle from Steve's conversation with his Son-In-Law last night.

"So I called David last night" Steve started. "I wanted to make sure he and Audrey (Steve's daughter) were OK considering the blizzard conditions in Denver." During that phone call David had decided to inform his Father-in-Law Steve, "You can't drive home from Iowa. Remember the blizzard?" and David continued to try to dissuade Steve. David explained we would be driving right into it as we traveled west. The blizzard would pick up moisture from the Gulf of

Mexico as it crosses into Kansas and Nebraska. With nothing but flatlands between us, by the time we reach the storm it would…, and David conclude with, "Gale-force winds; dumping snow by the foot; spreading highway wreckage and devastation of unseen proportion; and the WORLD AS WE KNOW IT WILL COME TO AN END!" apparently finishing at the same emotional peak my wife had finished at when I was back in Baltimore. Of course, Steve said to me, "David's my Son-In-Law – what does he know?" And we chuckled about David the Son-In-Law all the way to Omaha, Nebraska.

Our afternoon drive could not have been more pleasant. I remember two things about our drive across Nebraska. (And if you've ever driven across Nebraska then you know there's not much that stands out for the memory other than lots and lots of corn fields.) I distinctly remember a perfectly blue sky and bright sunshine that not only had totally dried the highway pavement, but was glittering off of every bush, tree, and telephone line we passed. You see, the Colorado blizzard had actually turned to freezing rain last night as it crossed into Nebraska. And then the storm turned north into South Dakota and on to Minnesota. We never hit it head on as the nay-sayers in our families had predicted. (They were so wrong in fact that they probably would qualify to be weathermen on Denver's TV stations – but that's a story for another time.)

So here were Steve and Gary, westbound on Interstate 80, driving across Nebraska in a bright, blue-sky December day, with the entire landscape decorated for the holidays in a beautiful, sparkling layer of ice that was lit up like a giant Christmas tree from the afternoon sunshine. Cake.

The second, vivid memory I have from this Nebraska crossing is how I accidentally tripped over a long-lasting and life altering idea with Steve. As I said before, we ran out of the usual small talk topics before we were out of Iowa. And we could only stay amused with stupid Son-In-Law jokes for so long.

By now even the satellite radio was no longer keeping my mind off of the fact that I was making a 30+ hour drive on about 5 hours of sleep. So it was somewhere near the Wahoo exit in Nebraska that two friends went into more serious topics of conversation about our lives, our aspirations, and other much deeper topics. I think Steve started it off, "Gary. Ever wish you had completed something you started in your life but is still unfinished?" Deep. "Well, I've always wanted to write a book" was my response. "Know anything about books?" I asked. Steve's response was the start of the life altering, right-turn in our friendship; in my life; and the catalyst for this story.

Steve proceeded to tell me about a book he had co-authored with a friend of his many years ago when they lived in Spokane, Washington. I believe they wrote it in the late 1980's. It was a book about how sales representatives can use a personal computer to increase their sales productivity. The title of his book was Double Your Sales Commission Using a Personal

<u>Computer</u>. Steve helped his co-author mostly by doing the editing, and, more importantly, Steve funded the whole project out of his pocket. Since it was Steve's money at stake, he also was responsible for finding a book publisher to buy the manuscript and publish the book. Steve ended with, "We didn't make any money, just broke even really, but it was a lot of fun. And, I have my name on the book!" He promised to find a copy for me, as he still had a few remaining copies stored at his house. I think Steve said the publisher made only one print run and it had been long since out of print. Deep.

"Steve, what if you helped me with my book project?" I asked. And I proceeded to tell Steve all about my dream of writing and publishing my book, <u>The Peace & Power of a Positive Perspective</u>. It's a collection of quotes and short stories that I have been accumulating since 1984. Ironically, I started this writing pursuit the year I entered the software marketplace as a salesman and began traveling regularly – like this trip I was on 20 years later. By the time we passed Ogallala, Nebraska and turned southwest off of I-80 onto I-76 heading towards the Colorado border, I had fully explained my book idea. When I asked, "So Steve, what do you think?" he replied without hesitation, "I'm in." A bit more decisive than yesterday's fire drill on whether he was coming with me on the road trip or not, yes? I went on, "Now Steve, I can't guarantee that this book idea will make us any money. But I can assure you now you won't have to fund any of the project. Just having you as a teammate would be perfect!" And then he said it. He said it with a smile and the confidence in his voice sealed the commitment we made right then and there in the middle of No-Where-Nebraska – "Gary, you can count on me; if I'm in for a penny, I'm in for a pound."

When we crossed into Colorado we hit the remnants of the blizzard. It was Friday, December 23rd, and the last leg of our journey from Sterling, Colorado to Littleton took more that twice as long as normal. The interstate was open, but snow-covered and icy. We drove the rest of the way home slowly and carefully and when we reached Steve's neighborhood, there was a narrow, rutted path on the side streets just wide enough for one car to drive down the middle of the street. I dropped Steve off at his house (we had called ahead, so Jacque was there already). I took the rented Oldsmobile home for the evening and returned it to Denver International Airport the following morning; Saturday, December 24th. The rental company charged me a $300 drop-off fee too. And when I took the rental shuttle to the airport terminal, I was the only one on the bus with a snow shovel and no luggage.

While everyone else on the bus was freaking out about how they were going to try to get home for Christmas, I just smiled; wondered how buried my car was at the airport parking lot; and reflected on the past 48 hours.

And this is the true story of how Steve and Gary made it home for Christmas. (And how this book came to be.)

Deep.

Preface:

<u>Why We Need Peace & Power in our Day</u>

May you feel peace & power today – and every day.

My day? It started with a missed wake-up call. I only had a few minutes to glance at the newspaper this morning. Bold headlines: "Market Down!"; "Unemployment Up!"; "Cost of Living Highest in a Decade"; "Today: Mostly Cloudy"; and "Cubs Lose Again". Certainly nothing I wanted to read about any further. Besides, I'm already running late for an "emergency meeting" with my boss. About what – I'm not quite sure.

I just spilled my McDonald's coffee in my lap as I pulled out of the drive-through. Not only will my stained dress pants look bad in front of my boss, but I don't think my private parts are burned enough to win a multi-million-dollar law suit. (There's never a little old lady around when you need one.) My wife just called, "The kids are sick."

A little music might be soothing (and lower my blood pressure). But no – the only thing on the radio is commercials; commercials on all eighteen FM stations and all twelve AM stations. What? Are the broadcasters in collusion to run their commercials at the same time? No station-hopping to find music? How do they do that? And, I accidentally left my iPod at home.

The car ahead of me has just been crawling for the past five miles. Finally, there's enough of a break in this heavy traffic where I can pass. Uh oh; the next sign I see is "Slow Down: Road Construction Ahead". I'm pretty sure I just broke a crown grinding my teeth!

So - How's your day?

"There is both peace and power in knowing and understanding who you are, where you're from and where you're going."

Doug Burgum

Is there any doubt that we could all use a little help in finding that inner peace and personal, self-confident power to carry us through our daily routine? After all, a positive attitude is priceless, yes?

I've been blessed to have been around rare combinations of peace and power almost my entire life. From my childhood, to participating in sports; the business world; from my family, friends, and acquaintances; I have observed and been impacted by great feats from famous, as well as everyday, people. In addition to Doug Burgum, former CEO of Great Plains Software, and his quote above, I have collected other quotes and short stories pertaining to living life motivated and confidently.

I was at Doug's key note speech to the Great Plains' worldwide resellers at the 2000 convention event in Fargo, North Dakota which they called "Stampede". (It was my first, and to-date, only trip to North Dakota.)

Doug was the very first person I heard use the phrase "peace and power" when talking about the balance we need in our business (and personal) life. And by no coincidence, his words were particularly applicable for the turn of the century.

In this book I write about Joe Newton, one of the most exceptional and successful high school boys' cross-country coaches of all time. "Tiger Joe", used foundation techniques of discipline, motivation, and positive thinking as the basis of his teams' string of successes over the span of more than 40 years. He was also a person I was lucky to know **before** – he was my brother's high school track coach in 1960; **during** – in my sophomore year, one of my best friends ran on the 1969 cross country team that finished 3rd in the Illinois High School State Meet. Ironically, that 3rd place finish prompted our high school Principal to cancel the planned celebration assembly on the Monday following the Meet. (York was favored to win.) And that decision prompted me to write my first and only article for the high school's newspaper, "Where have all the cheers gone?", when I questioned why a 3rd place finish in a competition of hundreds of high schools wasn't good enough in the eyes of our Principal to merit a celebration; and **after** – after my high school and college years, when I entered the business world to pursue a career in sales, I purchased all three of Joe Newton's books; several of his motivational tapes; and met with him from time-to-time to learn the "secrets" of his unparalleled winning ways. I found that these lessons-learned were totally applicable to my sales profession.

I write about my son Kevin. Kevin is a former high school rodeo cowboy and someone who possesses the rare combination of physical power, unbelievable courage, and the calm, polite demeanor of a true, gentle, man. I also write about my older son Eric and his daily struggle with the terrible affliction of Bi-Polar Disorder. Just facing each and every day requires him to have more courage and will power than anyone I know. Interestingly, he has coupled this disorder with a side of his personality that celebrates the tender love and pure devotion he has given to his pet dogs Ziggy and Chloe; to other "strays" he has taken in during his life; and to his Mom.

In my lifetime I have seen the devastation of the Vietnam War; the power of how the personal computer has changed our way of life; the end of apartheid; and the vivid symbol of peace when the Berlin Wall was torn down. In the 1980's I lived in Chicago during the glory years of "da Bears" and their Super Bowl victory in 1985, and the dynasty of Michael Jordan and "da Bulls". I've watched the passing of the moniker "Best Golfer of All Time" from Arnold Palmer to Jack Nicklaus to Tiger Woods.

I watched my Mom's great power, which she needed in order to deal with a new cancer treatment in the late 1960's that was so unimaginably harsh – that the administration of this treatment was solely based on the primitive science of trial and error – where the doctors' routine consisted of observing how much of a dose could she tolerate without dying from the treatment. It was an experimental treatment back then; offered only as a last resort for terminally ill cancer patients. This wasn't a cancer cure; just a radical option to extend one's life another year or two. It was due to her staying power (and that of many other patients like her) before she finally succumbed in 1974 that has helped pave the way to the development of the commonly used, life-saving cancer treatment we all know today as chemotherapy.

As a sales professional, I have carried a personal quota for over 30 years. And I can remember my 2nd full quota year as clearly as any. You see, in my first year as a sales rep, I was definitely more lucky than good. That led to a very nice promotion, and hefty quota increase for my second year – I was way over my head, in the deep end of the pool. After 26 weeks into my 52-week quota year, I was put on a "performance warning". At the 39th week, the Vice President of Sales was asking my Sales Manager to fire me. (By the way, at this time in my life, I was carrying a home mortgage; my first son Eric was five years old; and my wife and I decided it would be best if she focused fulltime raising our child vs. going back to work.) Since my company had chosen to proactively promote me (perhaps a bit prematurely) at the start of the year, I asked my Sales Manager to give me 52 weeks to sell my annual quota. We agreed that at the end of the 52nd week, if I was still below 100% of my assigned quota, I would resign.

At the end of my 51st sales week, I was at 75% of quota and significantly behind the required sales dollars necessary to reach 100%. However, I had been working hard on a few large accounts. At the 52nd weekly sales meeting, with the Vice President of Sales in attendance, I "roll-called" the second largest deal in the Region's history; finished my 2nd year at exactly 100% of my quota; and kept my job. Ironically, at that same company I went on to sell the two largest deals ever in the company's history, and 15 years later I recruited and led the most productive sales team in the nation. As of this writing, five of my former sales people are still there (14 years after my Sales Manager role came to an end) and are still high-performing producers who reach out to me for a bit of coaching from time-to-time.

One of these remaining five particularly stands out in my mind because of his demonstration of that rare combination of power with peace. Fred Ibrahim was then, and is to this day, the most powerfully polite sales professional I have ever known. His courteous manner almost single-handedly helps his prospective clients feel comfortable committing to the products and services he sells. His underlying competitive determination gets the rest of the sales job done. I don't think it's a coincidence that Fred also has a deep, personal conviction to his Christian faith.

This leads me to the last example in my lifetime of exposure to peaceful and powerful people. When I was twelve years old I was baptized by the Reverend Locke at Faith Community Church in Elmhurst, Illinois. That experience lit my eternal flame of Christianity that has burned in me everyday since.

So, let me wrap up by paraphrasing the late, great Pro Football player, Johnny Unitas (whom I quote again later in the book); and couple his profound statement with a few words of my own:

> **"Live today, and every day, to the fullest; with awe and enthusiasm; because when you die, you're dead for a long, long time."**

Life – R U In?

Book I: Road Warriors

Dedicated to the business professionals who travel; and the thoughts, hopes, and dreams that come to our mind at 30,000 feet while drinking a bad cup of coffee accompanied by a bag of 11 mini pretzels.

Not everyone can do this for a living.

Gary A. Pokorn

A key chain is a gadget that allows us to lose several keys at the same time.

Unknown

When you come to a fork in the road, take it.

Yogi Berra

Why are there interstate highways in Hawaii?

Unknown

It's on the path you do not fear that the wild beast catches you.

African Proverb

During a flight on a small airplane, the Flight Attendant asked a passenger if he would like to have dinner. "What are my choices?", the passenger asked. "Yes or No", the Flight Attendant replied.

Unknown

No matter how far you've gone down the wrong road, turn back.

Turkish Proverb

It does not matter how slowly you go, so long as you do not stop.

Confucius

As you exit the plane, please make sure to gather all of your belongings. Anything left behind will be distributed evenly among the Flight Attendants. Please do not leave children or spouses.

Unknown

Phillip's Law:

> Four-wheel drive just means getting stuck in more inaccessible places.

Unknown

Roger's Law:

As soon as the stewardess serves the coffee, the airliner encounters turbulence.

David's Explanation of Roger's Law:

Serving coffee on an aircraft causes turbulence.

Unknown

Not all those who wander are lost.

J.R.R. Tolkien

Eagles don't flock; you have to find them one at a time.

Ross Perot

Law of Life's Highway:

If everything is coming your way, you're in the wrong lane.

Unknown

Weather at our destination is 50 degrees with broken clouds; but they'll try to have them fixed before we arrive.

Unknown

Winfield's Dictum of Direction-Giving:

> The possibility of getting lost is directly
> proportional to the number of times the direction-
> giver says, *"You* can't miss it.*"*

Unknown

In calm waters, every ship has a good captain.

Swedish Proverb

Pilot: 'Folks, we have reached our cruising altitude
now, so I am going to turn the seat belt sign off. Feel
free to move about as you wish, but please stay inside
the plane 'til we land. It's a bit cold outside, and if you
walk on the wings it effects the flight pattern."

Unknown

If there is no wind, row.

Latin Proverb

After a particularly rough landing during thunderstorms
in Memphis, a Flight Attendant announced, "Please take
care when opening the overhead compartments because
after a landing like that, sure as hell everything has
shifted."

Unknown

From a Flight Attendant, "Welcome aboard our airline. To operate your seatbelt, insert the metal tab into the buckle, and pull tight. It works just like every other seatbelt and if you don't know how to operate one, you probably shouldn't be out in public unsupervised.

In the event of a sudden loss of cabin pressure, oxygen masks will descend from the ceiling. Stop screaming, grab the mask, and pull it over your face. If you have a small child traveling with you, secure your mask before assisting with theirs. If you are traveling with two small children, decide now which one you love more."

Unknown

Always…when there's a scenic route, take it. Arriving late and nasally challenged because you've mistakenly driven by the septic plant is still better than being punctual and bored.

Robert Fulghum

If you're not enjoying the journey, you probably won't enjoy the destination.

Joe Tye

All know the way. Few actually walk it.

Bodhidharma

Life's journey is not to arrive at the grave safely in a well preserved body, but rather to skid in sideways, totally worn out, shouting, Holy sh@#, what a ride!

Unknown

From the Pilot during his opening message:

> "We are pleased to have some of the best Flight Attendants in the industry. Unfortunately, none of them are on this flight."

Unknown

Part of a Flight Attendant's arrival announcement:

> "We'd like to thank you folks for flying with us today. And, the next time you get the insane urge to go blasting through the skies in a pressurized metal tube, we hope you'll think of us."

Unknown

Piloting your own plane may suggest a desire for freedom. It usually takes a lot of self-control, however, to earn the money necessary to buy your own plane. And once you are at the controls, concentration and rules are vital. Undisciplined pilots do not live long.

Alfred P. Sloan, Jr.

After a real crusher of a landing in Phoenix, the Flight Attendant got on the PA and said, "Ladies and gentlemen, please remain in your seats until Captain Crash and the crew have brought the aircraft to a screeching halt up against the gate. And, once the tire smoke has cleared and the warning bells are silenced, we'll open the door and you can pick your way through the wreckage to the terminal."

Unknown

Enjoy the ride. Knowing what you're doing is not a prerequisite to having fun doing it.

Gary A. Pokorn

There is a story about a little boy who was frightened coming aboard a famous cruise ship. He asked the first sailor he saw, "Sir, do ships this big sink very often?" "No", the sailor said, "only once."

Roger Smith

Learning is like rowing upstream; not to advance is to drop back.

Chinese Proverb

My Mom said she learned how to swim when someone took her out in the lake and threw her off the boat. I said, "Mom, they weren't trying to teach you how to swim."

Paula Poundstone

Riding: The art of keeping a horse between you and the ground.

Unknown

A famous Chairman of the Board of a national airline, uses self-deprecating humor, such as the story he told about a woman who wrote a letter complaining about his airline. She didn't like anything: not the peanuts, not the color of the plane. She didn't even like the uniforms of the stewards. She was just full of gripes.

The marketing division took it over, spent a week writing a 22-page letter trying to reason with her, and showed it to the Chairman before he signed it. He read it, and tossed it into the wastebasket. He asked for a piece of stationery and wrote; "Dear Madam, We're going to miss you.

Sincerely,
Herb"

Herb Kelleher

In riding a horse we borrow freedom.

Helen Thomas

The world looks wider from the back of a horse.

Unknown

You can tell a gelding; you can ask a stallion; but you must discuss it with a mare.

Unknown

My husband said if I don't sell my horses, he will leave me. Some days I miss him.

Unknown

People told Columbus the world was flat. He didn't insist it was round. He got in a boat.

3Com Advertisement

Even if you're on the right track, you'll get run over if you just sit there.

Will Rogers

The greatest thrill known to man isn't flying - it's landing.

Unknown

If you don't know where you're going, when you get there, you'll be lost.

Yogi Berra

The most important trip you may take in life is meeting people halfway.

Henry Boge

Greatness is a road leading towards the unknown.

Charles de Gaulle

Progress has less to do with speed and more to do with direction.

Unknown

…an airplane is merely a collection of spare parts flying in close formation…

Norman R. Augustine

The pessimist complains about the wind; the optimist expects it to change; the realist adjusts the sails.

William Arthur Ward

After every flight, pilots fill out a form called a gripe sheet, which conveys to the mechanics problems encountered with the aircraft during the flight that need repair or correction. The mechanics read and correct the problem, and then respond in writing on the lower half of the form what remedial action was taken, and the pilot reviews the gripe sheets before the next flight.

Never let it be said that ground crews and engineers lack a sense of humor. Here are some actual logged maintenance complaints and problems as submitted by pilots and the solution recorded by maintenance engineers.

(By the way, this airline is the only major airline that has never had an accident.)

P = The problem logged by the pilot.
S = The solution and action taken by the engineers

P: Left inside main tire almost needs replacement.
S: Almost replaced the inside main tire.

P: Test flight OK, except auto-land very rough.
S: Auto-land not installed on this aircraft.

P: Something loose in cockpit.
S: Something tightened in cockpit.

P: Dead bugs on windshield.
S: Live bugs on backorder.

P: Autopilot in altitude-hold mode produces a 200 feet per minute descent.
S: Cannot reproduce problem on ground.

P: Evidence of leak on right main landing gear.
S: Evidence removed.

P: DME volume unbelievably loud.
S: DME volume set to more believable level.

P: Friction locks cause throttle levers to stick.
S: That's what they're there for.

P: IFF inoperative.
S: IFF always inoperative in OFF mode.

P: Suspected crack in windshield.
S: Suspect you're right.

P: Number 3 engine missing.
S: Engine found on right wing after brief search.

P: Aircraft handles funny.
S: Aircraft warned to straighten up, fly right, and be serious.

P: Target radar hums.
S: Reprogrammed target radar with lyrics.

P: Mouse in cockpit.
S: Cat installed.

P: Noise coming from under instrument panel. Sounds like an elf pounding on something with a hammer.

S: Took hammer away from elf.

Unknown

The Lone Ranger and Tonto went camping in the desert. After their tent was set up, they fell sound asleep. One hour later, Tonto wakes the Lone Ranger and says, "Kemo-Sabe, look towards the sky. What do you see?" The Lone Ranger replies, "I see millions of stars." "What that tell you?" asks Tonto. The Lone Ranger ponders for a minute and then says, "Astronomically speaking, it tells me there are millions of galaxies and potentially millions of planets. Astrologically, it tells me that Saturn is in Leo. Time wise, it appears to be approximately a quarter past three in the morning. Theologically, it's evident the Lord is all-powerful and we are small and insignificant. Meteorologically, it seems we will have a beautiful day tomorrow. What's it tell you, Tonto?" Tonto is silent for a moment, then says, "Kemo-Sabe, you dumb a@#. Someone stole tent."

Unknown

Life in Chicago:

60° above -   Floridians wear coats, gloves and woolly hats.

Chicago people sunbathe.

50° above -   New Yorkers try to turn on the heat.

Chicago people plant gardens.

40° above -   Italian cars won't start.

Chicago people drive with their windows down.

32º above -   Distilled water freezes.

Lake Michigan's water gets thicker.

20° above -   Californians shiver uncontrollably.

Chicago people have their last cook-out before it gets cold.

15° above -   New York landlords   finally turn up the heat.

Chicago people throw on a sweatshirt.

Zero -   Californians fly away to Mexico.

Chicago people lick   the flagpole.

20° below -	People in Miami cease to exist.
	Chicago people get out their winter coats.
40° below -	Hollywood disintegrates.
	Chicago's Girl Scouts begin selling cookies door-to-door.
60° below -	Polar bears begin to evacuate Antarctica.
	Chicago's Boy Scouts postpone "Winter Survival" classes until it gets cold enough.
80° below -	Mt. St. Helen's freezes.
	Chicago people rent some videos.
100° below -	Santa Claus abandons the North Pole.
	Chicago people get frustrated when they can't thaw the keg.
297° below -	Microbial life survives on dairy products.
	Illinois cows complain of farmers with cold hands.

460° below -	ALL atomic motion stops.
	Chicago people start saying, "Cold 'nuff for ya?"
500° below -	Hell freezes over.
	The Cubs win the World Series!"

Unknown

One way to stop a runaway horse is to bet on him.

Unknown

Life is a marathon.

Larry Ellison

One wonders how we could survive without voices in our cars that keep reminding us that the door is open even when we want the door open to get some fresh air…

Norman R. Augustine

A ship in harbor is safe, but that is not what ships are built for.

John A. Shedd

The hardest thing to learn in life is which bridge to cross and which to burn.

David Russell

If you don't know where you are going, any road will get you there.

Turkish proverb

Even though we have admittedly fallen behind on the engine development,…, I feel confident that we will have the airplane's engine there for the first flight.

Norman R. Augustine

If you don't change your direction, you're likely to end up where you're headed.

Unknown

When I die, I want to die like my Grandfather who died peacefully in his sleep. Not screaming like all the passengers in his car.

Unknown

Airline Humor as seen on an Internet posting March 25, 2004.

All too rarely airline attendants make an effort to make the in-flight safety lecture and announcements a bit more entertaining. Here are some real examples that have been heard or reported:

On a flight with a major airline that has no assigned seating (you just sit where you want) passengers were apparently having a hard time choosing, when a Flight Attendant announced, "People, people we're not picking out furniture here, find a seat and get in it!"

On a flight with a very 'senior' Flight Attendant crew, the Pilot said, "Ladies and gentlemen, we've reached cruising altitude and will be turning down the cabin lights. This is for your comfort and to enhance the appearance of your Flight Attendants."

On a landing, the Flight Attendant said, "Please be sure to take all of your belongings. If you're going to leave anything, please make sure it's something we'd like to have.

Thank you for flying business express. We hope you enjoyed giving us the business as much as we enjoyed taking you for a ride."

Another Flight Attendant's comment on a less than perfect landing, "We ask you to please remain seated as Captain Kangaroo bounces us to the terminal."

Unknown

Welcome to Denver:

The morning rush hour is from 5:00 to 10:00 AM. The evening rush hour is from 3:00 to 7:00 PM. Friday's rush hour starts on Thursday.

Forget the traffic rules you learned elsewhere. Denver has its own version. The car or truck with the loudest muffler goes next at a 4-way stop. The truck with the biggest tires goes after that. Blue-haired, green-haired, or cranberry-haired ladies driving anything have the right of way all of the time.

North and South only vaguely resemble the real direction of certain streets. University and Colorado are two boulevards that run parallel. Geometry evidently not working at altitude, these streets intersect south of C470.

Highway 285 runs North, South, East and West and every direction in between; it can be found in every section of the Denver area making navigation very interesting. You can turn west onto southbound 285; you can turn north onto westbound C470; and you can drive southeast on the Northwest Parkway. This is why Denver uses the additional driving directions of "out", "up", "in", "down", and sometimes "over".

Construction barrels are permanent, and are simply moved around in the middle of the night to make the next day's drive more challenging. When you see an orange cone, you must stop and then move ahead slowly until there are no more cones. There need not be construction, just cones.

If someone has their turn signal on, wave them to the shoulder immediately to let them know it has been accidentally activated.

If it's 70 degrees, Thanksgiving is probably next week; if it's snowing, it's probably the weekend after Memorial Day.

If you stop at a yellow light, you will be rear-ended or cussed-out. A red light means four more cars can go through. Not three; not five. Four. Never honk at anyone. Ever. Seriously. Never yield at a "Yield" sign. The yield sign is like an appendix; it once had a purpose but nobody can remember what it was.

Just because a street on the east side of town has the same name as a street on the west side of town doesn't mean they're connected.

Unknown

Rene Augustine's Law of driving in unfamiliar environs:

> Attempting to read a roadmap while driving causes all traffic lights to turn green.
>
> Norman R. Augustine

Do more than you are paid for. There are never any traffic jams on the extra mile.

> Brian Tracy

A shared prayer from the Mayflower to the modern-day road warrior:

> We know before leavin'
>   The ride will be bumpy
>   The quarters will be dumpy
>   The stewards will be grumpy
>   And still we must go.
>
> We know before leavin'
>   The days will be long
>   ETAs promised will be wrong
>   Success smiles on only the strong
>   And still we must go.
>
> We know before leavin'
>   Our family will pine
>   We'll miss children's' prime
>   We barter money for time
>   And still we must go.

We know before leavin'
   To no one we sob
   While pursuing our job
   Our energy travels rob
   And still we must go.

We know before leavin'
   And we pray every evening
   Lord, get me home safe
   And I'll call the rest even.

                Gary A. Pokorn

Book II: Laws, Proverbs and Malarkey

Dedicated to those business professionals who know the difference between the smell of horse manure in the barn vs. the "sound" of horse manure in the office.

Not everyone can do this for a living.

Gary A. Pokorn

The problem with doing nothing is not knowing when you're finished.

Benjamin Franklin

20% of the people will be against anything.

Robert F. Kennedy

The main thing is to keep the main thing the main thing.

Unknown

Budget - noun; 1. A mathematical confirmation of your suspicions.

A.A. Latimer

Timing has a lot to do with the outcome of a rain dance.

Texas Bix Bender

Focused action beats brilliance any day.

Art Turock

The best parachute folders are those who jump themselves.

Unknown

One-half of our problems come from wanting our own way. The other half comes from getting it.

Unknown

Luck favors the persistent.

James C. Collins

Just when everyone is saying how great you are is when you're the most vulnerable.

Tom Connellan

To teach is to learn.

Japanese Proverb

A kind word warms for three winters.

Chinese Proverb

One of the advantages of being disorderly is that one is constantly making exciting discoveries.

A.A. Milne

Outside of a dog, a book is man's best friend. Inside a dog it is too dark to read.

Groucho Marx

Conscious - is when you are aware of something.

Conscience - is when you wish you weren't.

Unknown

A little neglect may breed great mischief; for want of a nail the shoe was lost; and for want of a shoe the horse was lost; and for want of a horse the rider was lost, being overtaken and slain by the enemy; all for want of a little care about a horse shoe nail.

Benjamin Franklin

Whether you think you can or think you can't, you're right.

Zig Ziglar

Fear makes the wolf bigger than he is.

German Proverb

An army of a thousand is easy to find; but, oh, how difficult to find a general.

Chinese Proverb

Time and I against any two.

Spanish Proverb

God did not create hurry.

Finnish Proverb

One with passion is better than forty who are merely interested.

Tom Connellan

Pratter's Prayer:

> Lord, make my words as sweet as honey, for tomorrow I may have to eat them.

Unknown

Good enough never is.

James C. Collins

The first and most important thing about goals is having one.

Geoffrey Albery

Many receive advice. Only the wise profit from it.

Publilius Syrus

All change is not growth, as all movement is not forward.

Ellen Glasgow

An expert is a man who has made all the mistakes which can be made in a very narrow field.

Niels Bohn

We do not understand:

Peace - until faced with conflict;

Trust - until we are betrayed.

Unknown

Kindness in words creates confidence.

Lao-Tzu

Murphy's Law:

If anything can go wrong, it will.

Unknown

Murphy's Law gives rise to Murphy's Philosophy:

Smile… tomorrow will be worse.

Unknown

Murphy's Paradox:

Doing it the hard way is always easier.

Unknown

Murphy's Sixth Corollary:

Whenever you set out to do something, something else must be done first.

Unknown

Murphy's Eighth Corollary:

It is impossible to make anything foolproof because fools are so ingenious.

Unknown

Addendum to Murphy's Law:

In precise mathematical terms, $1+1 = 2$, where "=" is a symbol meaning seldom if ever.

Unknown

Gattuso's Extension of Murphy's Law:

Nothing is ever so bad that it can't get worse.

Unknown

Bralek's Rule for Success:

Trust only those who stand to lose as much as you when things go wrong.

Unknown

Owen's Theory of Organizational Deviance:

Every organization has an allotted number of positions to be filled by misfits.

Unknown

J. Peed's Very General Law of Life in General:

If you wish it would, it won't; unless you don't, in which case it probably will.

Unknown

Law of Probable Dispersal:

Whatever hits the fan will not be evenly distributed.

Unknown

Harrison's Postulate:

For every action, there is an equal and opposite criticism.

Unknown

Hane's Law:

There is no limit to how bad things can get.

Unknown

A good beginning is half the work.

Irish Proverb

Naeser's Law:

You can make it foolproof, but you can't make it damn-fool-proof.

Unknown

Sweeney's Law:

>The length of a progress report is inversely proportional to the amount of progress.

>>Unknown

Just because everything is different, doesn't mean anything has changed.

>>Irene Peter

Because consumers are overwhelmed with data, they ignore or misunderstand most new concepts.

>>Seth Godin

Schnatterly's Summing Up of the Corollaries:

>If anything can't go wrong, it will.

>>Unknown

Nothing is easy to the unwilling.

>>Unknown

Allen's Law:

>Almost anything is easier to get into than to get out of.

>>Unknown

Goldenstern's Rules:

    1. Always hire a rich attorney.
    2. Never buy from a rich sales person.

            Unknown

Glaser's Law:

    If it says one size fits all, it doesn't fit anyone.

            Unknown

Seymore's Investment Principle:

    Never invest in anything that eats.

            Unknown

GAP's Reaction to Seymore's Investment Principle:

    Never buy anything that eats while you sleep.

            Gary A. Pokorn

Don't do something in a big way until you've seen it work in a small way.

            Anthony D'Andrea

Hershiser's Rule:

Anything labeled new and/or improved, isn't.

Unknown

Tissis' Organization Principle:

If you file it, you'll know where it is but never need it. If you don't file it, you'll need it but never know where it is.

Unknown

Sevareid's Law:

The chief cause of problems is solutions.

Unknown

Ringwald's Law of Household Geometry:

Any horizontal surface is soon piled up.

Unknown

Remember that not getting what you want is sometimes a wonderful stroke of luck.

Dalai Lama

Any fool can criticize, condemn, and complain - and most fools do.

Dale Carnegie

Never trust your dog to watch your food;

> Never tell your Mom her diet's not working.

> > Unknown

Kid wisdom:

> When your Dad is mad at you and asks you, "Do I look stupid?" Don't answer him.

> > Michael

The young are luckier:

> They don't need to remember what the rest of us are trying to forget.

> > Jan Carroll

What we've learned in the year 2000:

> Live contact will never be replaced by a machine (except ATM's - we love machines that give us money).

> > Jim Sterne

In every community, there is work to be done.
In every nation, there are wounds to heal.
In every heart, there is the power to do it.

> > Marianne Williamson

Grossman's Misquote of H.L. Mencken:

Complex problems have simple, easy-to-understand, wrong answers.

Unknown

Rudnicki's Nobel Principle:

Only someone who understands something absolutely can explain it so no one else can understand it at all.

Unknown

Maah's Law:

Things go right so they can go wrong.

Unknown

Tylczak's Probability Postulate:

Random events tend to occur in groups.

Unknown

Wolter's Law:

If you have the time, you won't have the money. If you have the money, you won't have the time.

Unknown

Farrell's Law of Newfangled Gadgetry:

The most expensive component is the one that breaks.

Unknown

Lampner's Law of Employment:

When leaving work late, you will go unnoticed. When leaving work early, you will meet your boss in the parking lot.

Unknown

Lovka's Law of Living:

As soon as you're doing what you want to be doing, you want to be doing something else.

Unknown

Law of the Lie:

No matter how often a lie is shown to be false, there will always be a percentage of people who believe it to be true.

Unknown

The Salary Axiom:

> The pay raise is just large enough to increase your taxes and just small enough to have no effect on your take-home pay.

> Unknown

Herblock's Law:

> If it's good, they discontinue it.

> Unknown

First Rule of Business:

> Having a detailed business plan doesn't guarantee success, but not having one guarantees failure.

> Unknown

Irish Blessing:

> May you never forget what is worth remembering, or remember what is worth forgetting.

> Unknown

The First Rule of Life:

> The best things in life aren't things.

> Unknown

Walt Disney's First Rule:

> If you can dream it, you can do it.
>
> Walt Disney

Finagle's Sixth Rule:

> Do not believe in miracles - rely on them.
>
> Unknown

Finagle's First Law:

> If an experiment works, something has gone wrong.
>
> Unknown

Red Skelton's First Rule:

> If we're having fun, the audience is having fun.
>
> Red Skelton

A straight flush is almost unbeatable in poker. But, as they said in the Old West; A Smith & Wesson beats a straight flush.

> Adam M. Brandenburger

May you live in interesting times.

> Chinese Proverb

Huns learn much faster when faced with adversity.

Wess Roberts

I can't understand why people are frightened by new ideas. I'm frightened by old ones.

John Cage

As Nietzsche said; "That which does not kill me, makes me stronger." Alas, he forgot to add; "That which kills me, kills me."

Jon Carrolle

What my Mother taught me:

My Mother taught me logic;
"Because I said so, that's why."

My Mother taught me irony;
"Keep laughing and I'll give you something to cry about."

My Mother taught me about the science of osmosis:
"Shut your mouth and eat your supper!"

Unknown

The charm of all power is modesty.

Louisa May Alcott

The most difficult thing in the world is to know how to do a thing and to watch someone else doing it wrong, without commentary.

T.H. White

The most terrifying thing is to accept yourself completely.

Carl Jung

Our fears are always more numerous than our dangers.

Seneca

Everyone should do two things each day that they hate to do, just for practice.

William James

Patience accomplishes its objective, while hurry speeds to its ruin.

Sa'di, Gulistan

Much is lost for want of asking.

Ronald M. Shapiro

To know that you do not know is the best

Lao-Tsu

The most skillful are those who practice the most.

Unknown

If we could sell our experiences for what they cost us, we'd all be millionaires.

Abigail Van Buren

Here's a test to find out whether or not your mission on earth is finished:

If you're alive, it isn't.

Richard Bach

Too much respect for problems kills faith in possibilities.

Unknown

Law Number XXXVII:

Ninety percent of the time things will turn out worse than you expect. The other 10 percent of the time you had no right to expect so much.

Norman R. Augustine

Good and quickly seldom meet.

Unknown

Do or do not. There is no try.

Yoda

Where you stand on an issue has a lot to do with where you sit.

Russ Deloach

It's what you learn after you know it all that counts.

Zig Ziglar

If you owe the bank $100, that's your problem. If you owe the bank $100 Million, that's the bank's problem.

John Paul Getty

New census figures show that 3 out of 4 people make up 75% of the world's population.

Unknown

You don't always get what you pay for. But you always pay for what you get.

Mark Twain

Without documentation, all routinized work turns into exceptions.

Michael E. Gerber

Parkinson's Law:

>Work expands so as to fill the time available for its completion.
>>Who said it –
>>>Historian C. Northcote Parkinson in a 1955 article in *The Economist.*
>>What it means –
>>>We can stretch any work to last as long as necessary.
>>What too many people think it means –
>>>We can compress any project into a shrinking schedule.
>>Why the difference matters –
>>>We can't squeeze into impossible schedules, no matter how loudly the executives scream.

Frank Hayes

Enough is better than too much.

Finnish Proverb

Facts do not cease to exist because they are ignored.

Aldous Huxley

Business is a place where everything we know how to do is tested by what we don't know how to do, and the conflict between the two is what creates growth.

Michael E. Gerber

Always do right! This will gratify some people and astonish the rest.

Mark Twain

Advice is what we ask for when we already know the answer but wish we didn't.

Emily Jong

The low bidder is usually someone who is wondering what he left out.

William Schreyer

Confession without repentance is just bragging.

Unknown

Do what's right and try to get along with people, in that order.

Ezra Taft Benson

The Paradox of Change:

The best time to do it is when it seems the least necessary.

David Cottrel

Experience is not what happens to you; it is what you do with what happens to you.

Aldous Huxley

Everything in the universe is subject to change and everything is right on schedule.

Unknown

Respect should be freely given and constantly earned.

Frank Altseiner

The 90-90 Rule of Project Scheduling:

The first 90% of the project takes 90% of the time, and the last 10% of the project takes the other 90% of the time.

Russell Kay

Make happy those who are near, and those who are far will come.

Chinese Proverb

Lord, help me be the man my dog thinks I am.

Unknown

The First Rule of Intelligent Tinkering:

Save all the parts.

Thomas L. Friedman

Pay what you owe and you'll know what is yours.

Benjamin Franklin

Nordstrom Rules:

Rule # 1 - Use your good judgment in all situations.

There will be no additional rules.

Bob Nelson

Endurance pierces marble.

Moroccan Proverb

Excerpts from Bill Gates' speech to Mount Whitney
High School, Visalia, CA:

Rule 1 - Life is not fair; get used to it.

Rule 4 - If you think your teacher is tough;
wait 'til you get a boss.

Rule 7 - Before you were born, your parents
weren't as boring as they are now.
They got that way from paying your
bills, cleaning your clothes and
listening to you talk about how cool
you thought you were. So before you
save the rain forest from the parasites
of your parents' generation, try
delousing the closet in your own room.

Rule 8 - Your school may have done away
with winners and losers, but life has
not. In some schools they have
abolished failing grades and they'll give
you as many times as you want to get
the right answer. This doesn't bear the
slightest resemblance to anything in
real life.

Rule 11 - Be nice to nerds. Chances are you'll
end up working for one.

Bill Gates

Barrack's Observation:

When the only tool you have is a hammer, you tend to see every problem as a nail.

Unknown

Grabel's Law:

Two is not equal to three - not even for very large values of two.

Russell Kay

The James J. Walker School of Management:

If you're there before it's over, you're on time.

Unknown

But one thing for sure; when you wrestle with a 500-pound gorilla, you rest when the gorilla wants to.

Unknown

Korman's Law:

The trouble with resisting temptation is it may never come your way again.

Unknown

In the beginning there was the Plan...

And then came the Assumptions.

And the Assumptions were without form.

And the Plan was without Substance.

And Darkness was upon the face of the
Workers.

And the Workers spoke among themselves
saying, "It is a crock of sh&! and it stinks."

And the Workers went unto their Supervisors
and said, "It is a crock of dung and we
cannot live with the smell."

And the Supervisors went unto their
Managers saying, "It is a container of
organic waste, and it is very strong, such that
none may abide by it."

And the Managers went unto their Directors,
saying, "It is a vessel of fertilizer, and none
may abide its strength."

And the Directors spoke among themselves,
saying to one another, "It contains that which
aids plant growth, and it is very strong."

And the Directors went to the Vice Presidents,
saying unto them, "It promotes growth, and
it is very powerful."

And the Vice Presidents went to the
President, saying unto him, "It has very
powerful effects."

And the President looked upon the Plan and
saw that it was good.

And the Plan became Policy.

And that is how sh&! happens.

Unknown

Love rules without rules.

Italian Proverb

Tell a man there are 300 billion stars in the universe and he'll believe you. Tell him the plate you're handing him is very hot and he'll have to touch it to believe it.

Mike Jaeger

Glasgow's Fourth Law:

> If it is so small it doesn't need documentation, then it doesn't do anything worthwhile.

Russell Kay

Work as if you will live a hundred years. Pray as if you would die tomorrow.

Benjamin Franklin

Those are my principles and if you don't like them, well, I have others.

Groucho Marx

Who would please everybody must rise early.

French Proverb

Reality is that stuff which, no matter what you believe, just won't go away.

David Paktor

Old age is like climbing a mountain. You climb from ledge to ledge. The higher you get, the more tired and breathless you become – but your views become more extensive.

Ingrid Bergman

Justifying a fault doubles it.

French Proverb

There is no distance on earth as far away as yesterday.

Robert Nathan

Don't judge each day by the harvest you reap, but by the seeds you plant.

Robert Lewis Stevenson

If the Hamm's Bear drank Schlitz, there'd be no land of sky-blue waters.

Unknown

Don't wait for the last judgment. It takes place every day.

Albert Camus

Book III: Dark Ages Computing ®

Observations on the automation of un-enlightened thinking.

Dedicated to those business professionals who know that just because something is technically feasible doesn't mean it's a good idea.

Not everyone can do this for a living.

Gary A. Pokorn

Conventional IT Wisdom:

- *Free* anything… isn't…
- If nobody else is trying something, there's usually a reason. Maybe not a good reason, but a reason…
- "We've never done it that way before" is a more powerful argument than any cost/benefit analysis...
- It always takes longer and costs more to do it later.
- A good idea is no match for a bad habit.
- The hardest problems get solved last.

Frank Hayes

Focus on the process, not on the product.

Rob Gilbert

Thing to say when you get caught sleeping at your computer:

- "Did you ever notice the sound that comes out of the keyboard when you put your ear real close?"
- Raise your head slowly and say, "In Jesus' name, Amen."

Unknown

God is in the details.

Mies van der Rohel

The universe is full of magical things patiently waiting for our wits to grow sharper.

Eden Phillports

Research is to see what everybody else has seen, and to think what nobody else has thought.

Albert Szent-Gzorgzi

Genius is nothing but a greater aptitude for patience.

Benjamin Franklin

The stages of Systems Development:

1. Wild enthusiasm
2. Disillusionment
3. Total confusion
4. Search for the guilty
5. Punishment of the innocent
6. Promotion of the non-participants

Arthur Black

I am a dot-com person, but my friend Steve, who works for a public television station, is a dot-org person. He believes dot-org persons are more noble than dot-com persons because dot-com persons are in businesses where they try to make money, while his dot-org public television station has a more lofty goal than making money: they would rather beg and whine for it.

Dan Danborn

As one IT Professional put it; "We've been reorganized, restructured, re-engineered, right-sized, down-sized, up-sized, TQM'ed, and MBO'ed, and if I hear the word empowered once more, I swear I'm gonna scream!"

Geoffrey James

At a recent annual meeting of the International Association of Clairvoyants, the meeting began by reading the minutes of next year's meeting.

Unknown

In general, I hate being connected, which I associate with being either interrupted or confused, not being in touch.

Geoffrey A. Moore

An organization's core competencies in one generation of technology can turn into core rigidities as far as the next is concerned.

Dorothy Leonard-Barton

First Law of Computer Programming:

Any given program, when running, is obsolete.

Unknown

GAP's Dictionary of Computereeze:

Bugs - Actually, we have no bugs; perhaps a few undocumented features, but definitely no bugs.

Gary A. Pokorn

I don't know why anyone would shell out lots of money for a computer game when you can have more fun and a greater challenge playing CSCP - Circumvent the Stupid Corporate Policy.

Dan Danborn

McChristy's Computer Axioms:

1. Back-up files are never complete.
2. Software bugs are correctable only after the software is judged obsolete by the industry.

Unknown

We always overestimate the change that will occur in the next two years and underestimate the change that will occur in the next ten.

Bill Gates

Manubay's Law for Programmers:

If a programmer's modification of an existing program works, it's probably not what the users want.

Unknown

Within a value network, each firm's competitive strategy, and particularly its past choice of markets, determines its perceptions of the economic value of a new technology. These perceptions, in turn, shape the rewards different firms expect to obtain through pursuit of sustaining and disruptive innovations. In established firms, expected rewards, in their turn, drive the allocation of resources toward sustaining innovations and away from disruptive ones. This pattern of resource allocations accounts for established firms' consistent leadership in the former and their dismal performance in the latter.

Clayton M. Christenson

As we often like to say about early software products, this system may be hard to use but at least it is slow.

Geoffrey A. Moore

Conventional IT Wisdom:

- Faster hardware doesn't solve business problems - unless the business problem is slow hardware.
- More bandwidth / memory / storage / processing power than you'll ever need, will last you six months. A year tops.
- IT project advance or die. Sometimes both. But if it isn't advancing it's dying.
- Functionality isn't the same as usefulness.
- The systems that last are the ones you were counting on to be obsolete.
- Exactly what you want, always costs more than you can afford.

- Data isn't information. Information isn't knowledge. Knowledge isn't manageable.

Frank Hayes

Opening remarks at the convention of psychics:

"All those who believe in telekinesis raise my hand."

Unknown

The game isn't about how good your products are; it's about how good you are at improving them. It isn't where you are; it's how fast you're moving. It isn't position; it's speed.

Adam S. Brandenburger

How you gather, manage, and use information will determine whether you win or lose.

Bill Gates

Technology supply may not equal market demand. The attributes that make disruptive technologies unattractive in established markets often are the very ones that constitute their greatest value in emerging markets.

Clayton M. Christenson

Klienbrunner's Corollaries:

If a programming task looks easy, it's tough. If a programming task looks tough, it's damn-well impossible.

Russell Kay

People without information cannot monitor themselves or make sound decisions. People with information can.

Ken Blanchard

Charismatic salespeople vie to win the attention of the visionary with outrageous promises, which heroic sales-support specialists try to illustrate in demos invented more or less on the fly, and which R&D groups agree to make come true under the influence of contagious enthusiasm and too much caffeine.

Geoffrey A. Moore

E-mail and voice-mail have, of course, exacerbated the problem in the last ten years. Unfortunately, for all their convenience, these innovations have made it much easier to believe we are communicating when we are merely informing; if I have e-mailed you, you know it. This presumption frequently escalates from knowledge to understanding, then to consent, and finally to the delusion of wisdom.

David S. Pottruck

Never let a computer know you're in a hurry.

Unknown

A knowledge worker is someone whose job entails having really interesting conversations at work.

Rick Levine

Masquerading as a better way to put everyone in touch, e-mail (and voice-mail) have become incessant distractions, a nonstop obligation and a sure source of stress and anxiety. I expect that a public statement by the Surgeon General is in the offering.

Seth Shostak

It is the system, not only the people, that will differentiate your business from everyone else's.

Michael E. Gerber

The collision of traditional business practices and Internet behaviors is creating the need to redefine what a client-vendor relationship is.

Gary A. Pokorn

Weinberg's Law:

If builders built buildings the way programmers wrote programs, then the first woodpecker that came along would destroy civilization.

Gerald M. Weinberg

Labor Rates

Regular	$	24.50
If you wait		30.00
If you watch		35.00
If you help		50.00
If you laugh		75.00

Unknown

Survival by Suicide:

How a company's pursuit of disruptive technology by spinning out an independent organization might entail, in the end, killing another of its business units.

Clayton M. Christensen

Moore's Law:

Transistor density on a manufactured semiconductor die doubles about every 18 months.

Who said it:

Intel Founder Gordon Moore, in a 1965 article for Electronics Magazine.

What it means:

Chip makers keep getting better at cramming transistors onto chips.

What too many people think it means:

Computers double their ability to get work done every 18 months.

Why the difference matters:

Transistor density doesn't equal the ability to get work done.

Gordon Moore

The majority of the problems in organizations are with systems, not people.

Stephen R. Covey

Professionals do not make decisions by opinions nor according to their preferences. They make them according to the facts.

Alfred P. Sloan

Since Appian was first a famous Roman highway, you'd think this might be a clue to Xymos' new identity. But the release says;

> "Appian was chosen for the name because it represents the ability to use leading edge technology and innovation, integrated into solutions that provide differentiation and competitive advantage."

Just what the Romans had in mind.

Rick Levine

If you have no data, you are just another person with an opinion.

George Eckes

It is not for nothing that Bill Gates likes to say that at Microsoft they know one thing: In four years, every product they make will be obsolete. The only question is whether Microsoft will make it obsolete or one of its competitors will.

Bill Gates

Re-engineering is like starting a fire in your head and putting it out with a hammer.

Louis V. Gerstner, Jr.

Gutterson's Law:

Any programming project that begins well ends badly. Any programming project that begins badly ends worse.

Russell Kay

Estimating Time:

To estimate the time required for any given project, first guess at the time you think it should take; multiply that number by 2 and change to the next higher unit-of-measure. Thus, if you think you can complete a project in one hour, tell your boss you will need two days; if four weeks, ask for eight months.

Russell Kay

Attract exciting people - more than a few of whom are a little offbeat.

Tom Peters

At the end of the day, in every industry, there's an integrator. Before the components reach the consumer, somebody has to sit at the end of the line and bring it all together in a way that creates value.

Louis V. Gerstner, Jr.

And along comes the Internet. It was as if we'd ordered it from Arizona: "Hello, US Federal Government? Yes, we'd like one totally open, high-speed, data backbone. Uh-huh, and charge that to the Department of Defense, why don't you? What's that? What do we want if for? Oh, just chatting about stuff. You know, this and that."

Rick Levine

Even a broken clock is right twice a day. Sometimes things go right by accident, and you are left with the dangerous illusion that it was your doing.

D. Michael Abrashoff

The established firms were, in fact, aggressive, innovative, and customer-sensitive in their approaches to sustaining innovation of every sort. But the problem established firms seem unable to confront successfully is that of downward vision and mobility. It was as if the leading firms were held captive by their customers, enabling attacking entrant firms to topple the incumbent industry leaders each time a disruptive technology emerged.

Clayton M. Christensen

Take the standard computer-industry press release. With few exceptions, it describes an announcement that was not made, for a product that was not available, quoting people who never said anything, for distribution to a list of people who mostly consider it trash.

Rick Levine

The difficult we do immediately. The impossible takes a little longer.

U.S. Army Corps of Engineers

What may go wrong

Implementation:
> People pay lip service to change, but are hard to wean from established practices.

How to prepare for it:
> Plan to remove old methods once the changes are introduced, so that there is no other option but to use the new methods.

> Robert Heller

There is nothing so useless as doing efficiently that which should not be done.

> Peter Drucker

You know you're living in 2004 when:

1. You accidentally enter your password on the microwave.
2. You haven't played solitaire with real cards in years.
3. You have a list of 15 phone numbers to reach your family of 3.
4. You email the person who works at the desk next to you.
5. When you make phone calls from home, you accidentally dial 9 to get an outside line.
6. You've sat at the same desk for four years and worked for three different companies.

7. Your boss doesn't have the ability to do your job.
8. Leaving the house without your cell phone, which you didn't have the first 20 or 30 (or 50) years of your life, is now a cause for panic and you turn around to go and get it.

Unknown

"Why not?" is a slogan for an interesting life.

Mason Cooley

The best students are those who never quite believe their professors.

Jim Collins

The first rule of any technology used in a business is that automation applied to an efficient operation will magnify the efficiency. The second is that automation applied to an inefficient operation will magnify the inefficiency.

Bill Gates

Two types of uncertainty plague most efforts to introduce major new products: known-unknowns and unknown-unknowns.

Norman R. Augustine

The truth is, there's nothing new about being in a new economy. Those who faced the invention of electricity, the telephone, the automobile, the radio, or the transistor - did they feel it was any less of a new economy than we feel today?

Jim Collins

Due to recent cutbacks the light at the end of the tunnel will be turned off until further notice.

Unknown

Never trust a computer you can't throw out a window.

Steve Wozniak

Building computers isn't so hard, but making them work is something else again.

Gary Anthes

The Know-Nothing:

> This is that clueless user who looks in vain for the "Any Key" when his computer prompts him to "Hit Any Key."

Lisa DiCarlo

The apocryphal story of the gentleman who, lacking any cheese, baited his mousetrap with a picture of some cheese. To his acute disappointment, he is said to have caught a picture of a mouse.

Norman R. Augustine

I love deadlines… I like the whooshing sound they make as they go by.

Douglas Adams

According to an article in the Wall Street Journal, a 1996 survey of 360 companies by the research firm Standish Group International found that 42 percent of corporate information technology projects were abandoned before completion.

Unknown

GAP's Dictionary of Computereeze:

Salesman - A user-friendly conveyor of highly technical, data processing concepts in an easy-to-understand, though sometimes slightly inaccurate fashion.

Gary A. Pokorn

There are those individuals, both outside the federal government and inside, who are endowed with that special talent to take fairly lucid concepts and, through subtle embellishment, make them very nearly incomprehensible.

Norman R. Augustine

Lightweight managers can effectively run projects, even technologically complex platform projects, as long as the individuals and groups within the organization know how to work together because new modules can be plugged and played in the established architectural system.

It also demonstrates that even technologically straight forward projects may require heavyweight teams when individuals and groups within the organization are required to work together in different ways, on different problems, and at different times in the project than had been customary.

Clayton M. Christensen

Arguing with an engineer is like wrestling a pig in the mud. After a few hours you realize, the pig likes it.

Unknown

Book IV: Seers, Sooth Sayers, & Committees

Dedicated to the business professionals who suffer through the "wisdom" of theoretical and impractical advice, all of the while praying.

Not everyone can do this for a living.

Steve Whitehead

A committee is twelve men doing the work of one.

John F. Kennedy

It is amazing what you can accomplish if you do not care who gets the credit.

Harry S. Truman

People can be divided into three groups:

1. Those who make things happen,
2. Those who watch things happen, and
3. Those who wonder what's happening.

Unknown

One of the greatest difficulties encountered by corporate entrepreneurs has been finding the right beta test sites where products could be interactively developed and refined with customers. Generally, a new venture's entrée to the customer was provided by the salesperson representing the firm's established product lines. This helped the firm develop new products for established markets but not to identify new applications for new technology.

Clayton M. Christensen

ACTION:

> Having the world's best idea will do you no good unless you act on it. People who want milk shouldn't sit on a stool in the middle of a field in hopes that a cow will back up to them.

Curtis Grant

A decision is what people make when they can't find anyone to serve on a committee.

Unknown

Kirby's Comment on Committees:

A committee is the only life form with 12
stomachs and no brain.

Unknown

As far as I can tell, every layer of management exists for
the sole purpose of warning us about the layer above.

Scott Adams

"Is there any reason you could not serve as a juror on
this case?" the judge asked the junior executive called
for jury duty. "I don't want to be away from my job that
long, answered the prospective juror." "Can't they do
without you?" the judge probed. "Sure, said the up-and-
comer. But I don't want them to know that."

Unknown

They planned to fail early and inexpensively in the
search for the market for a disruptive technology. They
found that their markets generally coalesced through an
iterative process of trial, learning, and trial again.

Clayton M. Christensen

In the marketplace, it's the party with the power who gets to make the rules.

Barry Nalebubb

Your managers don't simply manage people; your managers manage the System by which your business achieves its objectives.

Michael E. Gerber

"What's your opinion of my idea?" the brash young man asked his boss. "It isn't worth anything", said the boss. "I know", conceded the young egotist, "but give it to me anyway."

Unknown

If you don't set specific expectations, don't expect much.

Unknown

People are not your most important asset. The right people are.

Jim Collins

My policy is to have no policy.

Abraham Lincoln

In the story Silver Blaze, Sherlock Holmes is called in to investigate the mysterious disappearance of the Wessex Cup favorite just a few days before the big race. Evidently someone has crept into the stables and abducted the horse. But who? And how did he elude the dog guarding the stables?

> Inspector Gregory:
> "Is there any other point to which you would wish to draw my attention?"
>
> Sherlock Holmes:
> "To the curious incident of the dog in the night-time."
>
> Inspector Gregory:
> "The dog did nothing in the night-time."
>
> Sherlock Holmes:
> "That was the curious incident."
>
> Unknown

The simple truth about the greatest business people I have known is they have a genuine fascination for the truly astonishing impact little things done exactly right can have on the world.

> Michael E. Gerber

That Mary is the Under-Vice President of Expectation Deflations for the western semi-region tells you nothing. That Mary is wicked smart, totally frank, and a trip to work with tells you everything.

Rick Levine

A camel is a horse designed by a committee.

Norman R. Augustine

At first speechless, Acheson had said he was not qualified to meet the demands of the office. "This", responded Truman, "was undoubtedly so, the question was whether he would do the job."

Harry S. Truman

In all my years in business, I have found that people in meetings tend to agree on decisions that as individuals, they know are dumb.

John M. Capozzi

Dissent, even conflict, are necessary, are indeed desirable. Without dissent and conflict there is no understanding. And without understanding, there are only wrong decisions.

Alfred P. Sloan Jr.

Rein in Chaos:

> Clarity of direction, which includes describing
> what we are going after as well as what we will
> not be going after, is exceedingly important at the
> late stage of a strategic transformation.

Andy Grove

None of us is as smart as all of us.

Warren Benzis

In a visit to a utility company to study its best practices,
teams from Sprint Corporation in Westwood, Kansas,
were shocked to learn that some corporate cultures
weren't quite as rigid as theirs. When the Sprint teams
asked questions regarding dress code and attendance
policies, the firm responded that its policies were come
to work, and wear clothes.

Bob Nelson

Let's make a small number of rules, really enforce them,
and then create an environment in which people can
fulfill their own potential.

Thomas L. Friedman

It is important to realize what the purpose of these debates is and what it isn't. Don't think for a moment that at the end of such debates all participants will arrive at a unanimous point of view. That's naïve. However, through the process of presenting their own opinions, the participants will define their own arguments and facts so that they are in much clearer focus. Gradually, all parties can cut through the murkiness that surrounds their arguments, clearly understand the issues and each other's point of view. The clearer images that result permit management to make a more informed - and more likely correct - call.

Andy Grove

In its most fundamental sense, execution is a systematic way of exposing reality and acting on it. Most companies don't face reality very well.

Larry Bossidy

In overcoming resistance, prevention is better than cure.

Robert Heller

He defines a committee as group of the unwilling, picked from the unfit, to do the unnecessary.

Richard Harkness

"We have the hardest working steel workers in the world", said one Nucor executive. "We hire five, work them like ten, and pay them like eight."

Jim Collins

Corporate Staff:

Known in some quarters as Sea Gulls for reasons relating to their propensity to fly round the country leaving their mark wherever they have alighted.

Norman R. Augustine

We're into the era where a committee designs airplanes. You never do anything totally stupid, you never do anything totally bright. You get an average, wrong answer.

Kelly Johnson

The purpose of bureaucracy is to compensate for incompetence and lack of discipline - a problem that largely goes away if you have the right people in the first place.

Jim Collins

Respect for hands-on knowledge wins over respect for abstract authority.

Rick Levine

Rules:

> There ain't no rules here. We're trying to accomplish something.

Thomas Edison

The amount of time devoted to the debate of a subject is inversely proportional to the importance of the outcome.

Norman R. Augustine

Alfred Sloan, Chairman and CEO of General Motors for years was in a Board meeting about to make an important decision. He said, "I take it that everyone is in basic agreement with this decision." Everyone nodded. Sloan looked at the group and said, "Then I suggest we postpone the decision. Until we have disagreement, we don't understand the problem."

Alfred Sloan

A consultant is someone who saves his client almost enough to pay his fee.

Arnold H. Glasgow

My greatest strength as a consultant is to be ignorant and ask a few questions.

Peter Drucker

The mark of a true M.B.A. is that he is often wrong but seldom in doubt.

Robert Buggell

Being wrong is a lot funnier than being right. Laughter is the sound that knowledge makes when it's born.

Rick Levine

It nonetheless spoke highly of the firm's management that they seemed to be going out of business in an orderly fashion.

Norman R. Augustine

Look for the ridiculous in everything and you will find it.

Jules Renard

Another mystery commonly observed by committee pathologists is that the time consumed in debate is dominated by those with the least to offer.

Norman R. Augustine

Clock building, not time telling; be a clock builder - an architect - not a time teller.

Jim Collins

Bad news does not improve with age.

D. Michael Abrashoff

Nothing is impossible. Some things are just less likely than others.

Jonathan Winters

Prepare:

It wasn't raining when Noah built the ark.

Howard Ruff

Answering the unasked question, what someone really wants to know - that's a really special skill.

Unknown

People who read me seem to be divided into four groups; Twenty-five percent like me for the right reasons; 25 percent like me for the wrong reasons; 25 percent hate me for the right reasons. It's the last 25 percent that worries me.

Robert Frost

My opinion may have changed, but not the fact I'm right.

Unknown

When in doubt:

Mumble.

Fiorello LaGuardia

The truth, however, is that virtually all well-established strategy models work well in some situations and cause failure in others, so the real skill is less in knowing the strategy than in sorting out the situations to which it actually applies.

Unknown

Chieftains must inspect their Huns frequently in order to see that what is accomplished meets with what is expected.

Wess Roberts

To the government, cutting red tape often means slicing it into long strips lengthwise.

Norman R. Augustine

The greatest secret of success in life is for a person to be ready when their opportunity comes.

Benjamin Disraeli

Emotion cannot be countered by reason alone, but requires emotional reassurance.

Robert Heller

Whatever a company's culture is, that is the true teacher. Culture trains.

Linda Richardson

We must never fail to analyze the past. No bleached bone of a battle-lost Hun must go unnoticed as we prepare for the future by laying aside the ill-conceived and undisciplined strategies of our past.

Wess Roberts

Good pitching will always stop good hitting and visa versa.

Casey Stengel

Research has shown, in fact, that the vast majority of successful new business ventures abandoned their original strategy when they began implementing their initial plans and learned what would and would not work in the market.

The dominant difference between successful ventures and failed ones, generally, is not the astuteness of their original strategy. Guessing the right strategy at the onset isn't nearly as important to success as conserving enough resources so that new business initiatives get a second or third stab at getting it right.

Those that run out of resources or credibility before they can iterate toward a viable strategy are the ones that fail.

Clayton M. Christensen

"How many of you went to the same place on vacation more than once?" Only a few hands went up. He went on, "and how many of you went on vacation to the same place four times or more?" No hands were raised.

"You see", said the consultant, "it's not true that people don't like change. When we are left to do the choosing, we all like a certain amount of variety and change in our lives."

Unknown

It seems to me that the largest impediment to a healthy attitude toward failure is our inability to distinguish between just plain being stupid and failing on the way to great success.

Unknown

There are always some fleas a dog can't catch.

Abraham Lincoln

If your business depends on you, you don't own a business - you have a job. And it's the worst job in the world because you're working for a lunatic!

Michael E. Gerber

If you're given a choice between bringing in a consultant or beer, choose the beer.

Rick Levine

Strategic plans sound like a political speech. Strategic actions are concrete steps.

Andy Grove

Change respects no boundaries, traditions or history of accomplishments.

Richard W. Oliver

It's better to be prepared for an opportunity and not have one than to have an opportunity and not be prepared.

Whitney Young

A strategy built for an organization that cannot execute it is not a good strategy.

Chris Zook

"I must do something", will always solve more problems than, "Something must be done."

Unknown

We have statistics but no understanding. And understanding is not more or higher information.

Rick Levine

The significant problems we face cannot be solved by the same level of thinking that created them.

Albert Einstein

Nobody is in a rush for the wrong answer.

Robert D. Cohen

It takes humility to seek feedback. It takes wisdom to understand it, analyze it, and appropriately
act on it.

Stephen R. Covey

Almost everything comes from almost nothing.

Henri Frederic Amiel

The problem with risk is that it is… risky. The extent of risk can sometimes be quantified but the fact is that when the calculation is completed, there is an irreducible element of luck involved when a risk is taken.

Alfred P. Sloan Jr.

Change frightens workers, and their fears thrive in silence. The antidote is obvious:
Keep talking.

D. Michael Abrashoff

Experience is something I always think I have until I get more of it.

Dan Kaercher

"Consul", n:

> In American politics, a person who having failed to secure an office from the people is given one by the Administration on condition that he leave the country.

> Ambrose Bierce

A decision is the action an executive must take when he has information so incomplete that the answer does not suggest itself.

Arthur W. Radford

When you don't know what to do, walk fast and look worried.

Paul Dickson

No organization is so screwed up that somebody doesn't like it as it is.

Price Pritchett

The trouble with the future is that it usually arrives before we're ready for it.

Arnold H. Glasow

I had hoped to follow the advice of all the management gurus and try to avoid making major decisions in the first ninety days, but that only happens in guru world.

Louis V. Gerstner, Jr.

Those who do not plan end up working for those who do.

Roger Smith

All good work is done in defiance of management.

Bob Woodward

The hard stuff is easy. The soft stuff is hard. And the soft stuff is a lot more important than the hard stuff

Dr. Tom Malone

Man's biggest mistake is to believe that he's working for someone else.

Nashua Cavalier

Put your best people on your biggest opportunities, not your biggest problems.

Jim Collins

Building Trust

Resistance to change takes three main forms:

- Opposition based on misunderstanding or rational objections
- Fear of personal consequences
- And emotional distrust

The intensity of negative response will largely depend on the existing degree of distrust.

Robert Heller

One thing that tells me a company is in trouble is when they tell me how good they were in the past.

Michael Hammer

We don't think ourselves into a new way of acting; we act ourselves into a new way of thinking.

Larry Bossidy

Since by definition, new ideas don't have metrics, the result is that great ideas tend to be stillborn in major corporations today.

D. Michael Abrashoff

You can see a lot by observing.

Yogi Berra

I find there is a profound difference in what I find interesting and what I find important.

Ann E. Organist

It seems to me that no soothsayer should be able to look at another soothsayer without laughing.

Cicero

Why are there more flies in Cairo than lobbyists in Washington? Answer: Cairo got first choice.

Norman Augustine

If all the world's economists were laid end to end, they would not reach a conclusion.

George Bernard Shaw

Make three correct guesses consecutively, and you will establish a reputation as an expert.

Lawrence Peter

Task forces are usually led by, if not composed of, people from outside the organization, so they will not be tainted by existing biases. It frequently happens that they are not tainted by any relevant experience, either.

Frank Carlucci

It is easy to see problems; solutions are tougher.

Robert C. Anderson

Reality is that which when you stop believing in it, doesn't go away.

Philip K. Dick

One can either face reality at the outset or one can disseminate the bad news on the installment plan.

Norman Augustine

A company should never outsource its eyes. There is simply no substitute for seeing for yourself.

W. Chan Kim

When everyone is against you, it means that you are absolutely wrong – or absolutely right.

Albert Guinar

A little experience upsets a lot of theory.

S. Parkes Cadman

The next best thing to being wise oneself is to live in a circle of those who are.

C.S. Lewis

Most of the managers of companies that enjoy transitory success assume that tomorrow will be more or less like today; that significant change is unlikely, is predictable, and in any case will come slowly.

Richard Foster

A consultant is an individual handsomely paid for telling senior management of problems, about which senior management's own employees have told the consultant.

Norman Augustine

It is not enough to have a good mind. The main thing is to use it well.

Rene Descartes

In order for companies to survive a discontinuity they must, as Harvard Business Review editor Alan M. Kantrow once put it, face the rather unpalatable reality that there may have to be fundamental changes in who they are, what they do and how they do it.

Alan M. Kantrow

Lewis Thomas, president of the Sloan-Kettering Cancer Institute; A good way to tell how the work is going is to listen in the corridors. If you hear the word "Impossible!" spoken as an expletive, followed by laughter, you will know that someone's orderly research plan is coming along nicely.

Lewis Thomas

But all things finally began to move when the threat of help from headquarters was received.

Norman Augustine

Just because we can't understand the purpose of things, however insignificant, doesn't mean that there is none.

Abraham Lincoln

1st **Intermission**

Dedicated to creative problem-solving:

Bill Pless brought his daughter's third grade math homework to the office to see how his sales team did in answering the problem. See how you do.

Your assignment is to place 9 pigs in the 8 pens (below). No pen can have more than 1 pig placed in it; no pig can be left out of the pens. The configuration of the pens cannot be changed. Your design of the pigs is not important.

The pens:

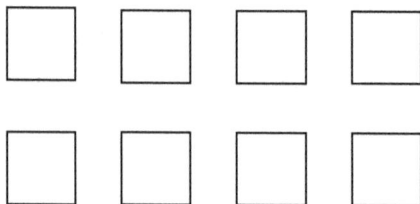

Unknown

Not everyone can do this for a living.

Gary A. Pokorn

Book V: Money Talks - Chocolate Sings

Dedicated to the knights of business. Not everyone can do this for a living.

Gary A. Pokorn

"The Noble Art"

Salespeople Are the Knights of Business

With permission - by Scott DeGarmo

Just why does SUCCESS say this issue is devoted to the "noble art of selling?

As many a salesperson says when hit between the eyes with a question, "I'm glad you asked that." (The response is no mere throwaway phrase. It gives me a chance to show enthusiasm and buys a moment to think of an answer.)

And so, now that you've thought – why NOBLE? And why ART?

First, the occasion calls for some exalted banner, as this is the *only* issue of the year we dedicate entirely to a single topic.

Beyond that, noble means pre-eminent and selling is the pre-eminent business skill. You can have every other element in place, but without sales you have nothing. A Dun & Bradstreet study of the cause of business failure puts "inadequate sales" at the top of the list.

Noble also means "of the nobility", and salespeople are the knights of business. While their colleagues skulk about the castle, salesmen and saleswomen get out there and make results happen in the real world.

Like the noble knight, the salesperson has a mission, a crusade. Belief in his product is his creed. He knows it can work miracles for his customers. He venerates his mission, aware that the more he learns about what he is selling, the more he can believe in it – and the more he believes in it, the more convincing he will be. Not only does he collect great sales stories, he learns the best way to tell them (see our list of the 10 most powerful types of sales stories, page 14).

One who is noble is above petty concerns. Salespeople act nobly when they keep their eyes on the goal despite the most ghastly frustrations. Where mere commoners would react with anger, resentment, or dismay, the noble salesperson has the inner steel to be gracious and the ruthless resolve to remain ever sensitive to the client's needs. His concentration doesn't waver when he is under attack. Ego never gets in his way. When necessary, he adroitly sacrifices real or perceived power in order to move the sale forward.

You mean he kowtows. Well, so much for noble. What about art?

If he kowtows, it is with consummate skill. To say something is an art means it requires prowess and mastery to execute. So the salesperson hones every aspect of his performance – rehearsing, refining, scheming late into the night.

Whatever is an art is also beyond the ability of another to fully dissect or reduce to a formula. It smacks of individual virtuosity and creativity.

It's best when you don't actually *see* the art involved in selling (as noted in our piece, "The Art of Selling," page 30). The individual actions of a salesperson, taken separately, may appear outwardly unremarkable. Yet, the unseen talent used to weave together all the countless elements of a sale may be so ingenious as to …

Go on. You seem a bit choked up.

…as to make the mind quiver with delight. Scientists use the word "elegant" to describe their experiments, meaning they have no wasted steps. Selling can be elegant in this sense when it concentrates the energy of the salesperson, when it eliminates needless activity in the selling process. Salespeople can be brilliant at stitching together a day of phone calls, lunches, presentations, and follow-up letters. The casual banter that elicits a piece of vital information can be a master stroke. What a shame when salespeople are badgered and second-guessed by pettifogging managers, who could be much more effective if they encouraged, assisted, and pointed the way.

A poem we once published had thoughts along the following lines: A salesperson must have the quickness of an athlete, the fluency of an orator, the flair of an actor, the courage of a warrior, the acumen of a litigator, the insight of a psychiatrist, and the endurance of a saint.

I'm sold. I want to read about selling NOW."

Market Terminology for Dummies:

Bull Market - A random market movement causing the investor to mistake himself for a financial genius.

Momentum Investing - The fine art of buying high and selling low.

Standard & Poor - Your investment strategy in a nutshell.

Mailbits.com

The real challenge of selling stuff online is in the selling, not in the technology.

Seth Godin

Sales forces, like any other channel of distribution, will optimize for their own benefit.

Geoffrey Moore

Saving is greater than earning.

German Proverb

Learning sales tasks is easy; learning selling skills is hard.

Gary A. Pokorn

What do most sales people do when they don't know what to do?

Unknown

Ralph Waldo Emerson's First Rule of Money:

Money often costs too much.

Ralph Waldo Emerson

A legacy of the old advertising industry adage - if you have nothing to say, sing it.

Rick Levine

Before you can sell them your full solution, you first must establish a business relationship. Otherwise, it's just a money-decision.

Gary A. Pokorn

A good business manager hires optimists as salesmen and pessimists to run the credit department.

Unknown

When I first started working I used to dream of the day when I might be earning the salary I'm starving on now.

Unknown

There are some men who, in a fifty-fifty proposition, insist on getting the hyphen too.

Lawrence J. Peter

It is especially hard to work for the money you've already spent for something you didn't need.

Unknown

Cold calling is a numbers game (or, to be more precise, a ratios game).

Stephen Schiffman

You make the sale when the prospect understands that it will cost more to do nothing about the problem than to do something about it.

Ben Feldman

It's not the cheaper things
That we want to possess
But expensive things
That cost a little less.

Rolf B. White

Differentiation loses its meaning when the features and functionality have exceeded what the market demands.

Clayton M. Christenson

DETERMINATION:

I remember when I was first starting out and asking a colleague I respected how many sales calls he would make on a prospect before giving up. He told me, "It depends on which one of us dies first."

Harvey Mackay

How to have a Winning Day:

    1. You have to listen more than you talk…
    3. You have to smile more than you frown…
    10. You have to be fascinated more than
        you're frustrated…
    15. You have to believe in yourself more than
        you doubt yourself.
    16. You have to work more than you whine.
    17. You have to do more than you don't.

                  Rob Gilbert

Getting more volume from each account - think share of customer instead of just share of market.

                  Ronald Shapiro

Clarity of expectations is a sales person's #1 motivator.

                  Gary A. Pokorn

Because emerging markets are small by definition, the organizations competing in them must be able to become profitable at small scale. This is crucial because organizations that are perceived as being profitable and successful can continue to attract financial and human resources...

                  Clayton M. Christenson

Permission Marketing is:

> Anticipated - people look forward to hearing
> from you
> Personal - the messages are directly related
> to the individual
> Relevant - the marketing is about something that
> person is interested in.

Seth Godin

To assess your added value, you have to put yourself in
the other player's shoes and ask what you bring to them.

Barry J. Nalebuff

Charles Revlon, the founder of Revlon and an
extraordinarily successful entrepreneur, once said about
his company: "In the factory Revlon manufactures
cosmetics, but in the store Revlon sells hope."

Charles Revlon

Even a bad interruption campaign gets some results
right away, while a permission campaign requires a
belief in the durability of the permission concept before
it blossoms with success.

Seth Godin

Five ways to double your income:

1. Double the number of cold calls you make
2. Get through more often
3. Get more appointments
4. Close more sales
5. Generate more dollars per sale.

Stephen Schiffman

From a sales point of view, there is really only one drawback to Techies: they don't have any money.

Geoffrey Moore

A billion here, a billion there, pretty soon it adds up to real money.

Senator Everett Dirksen

The Law of the Marketplace:

If only one price can be obtained for any quotation, the price will be unreasonable.

Unknown

The ability to see the situation as the other side sees it, as difficult as it may be, is one of the most important skills a negotiator can possess.

Barry J. Nalebuff

A marketer who has achieved intravenous permission from his customer is making the buying decisions on behalf of the customer. The privilege is huge, but the downside is significant. If the marketer guesses wrong or, worse, abuses the permission, it will be cancelled in a heartbeat.

Seth Godin

The only money that counts is the customers'.

Geoffrey Moore

What's my return on investment in e-commerce? Are you crazy? This is Columbus in the New World. What was his ROI?

Andrew Grove

An angry worker goes into her company's payroll office to complain that her paycheck is $50 short. The payroll supervisor checks the books and says, "I see here that last week you were overpaid by $50. I can't recall your complaining about that." "Well, I'm willing to overlook an occasional error, but this is two in a row."

Paul Dickson

The commodity is cosmetics; the product is hope.

Charles Revlon

Some of the essential principals of tornado marketing:

1. Attack the competition ruthlessly.
2. Expand your distribution channel as fast as possible.
3. Ignore the customers.

Geoffrey Moore

Sign on a fence:

Salesmen welcome - dog food is expensive.

Unknown

Time isn't money, after all - it's more personal and more important. Once I asked a friend to help me with a project, and I added, "Of course, I'll pay you for your time." He smiled, "I'm afraid your money is a poor substitute for my time."

Floyd Allen

Remember, in selling situations only one bad thing can happen - only one - and that is it can take a long time to lose.

Robert B. Miller

Contrary to the novelized, fictionalized, and Hollywoodized version of mythic moguls and the big-bucks business world, deal-making shouldn't be a stare-down in a stud poker game, a shoot-out at the OK Corral, hand-to-hand combat, a high-tech military maneuver, or an all-out atomic war. Despite the macho, swaggering, in-your-face lingo - winner take all, out for blood, call their bluff, raise the stakes, battle-scarred, make 'em beg for mercy, first one to blink, an offer they can't refuse, make 'em meltdown, go for the kill, last man standing - negotiation isn't about getting the other side to wave a flag and surrender. Negotiation is not war.

Ronald Shapiro

The biggest challenge to tracking segment revenues is post-sale revision of the target or bull's-eye marketing, where you draw a bull's-eye target around whatever you actually hit.

Geoffrey Moore

Real charity doesn't care if it's deductible or not.

Unknown

Most sales people think that selling is closing. It isn't. Selling is opening.

Michael E. Gerber

Despite all the clinical, logical, rational, psychological, data-sifting analysis, graphs, pie-charts, methods, and techniques from MBA's, CPA's, CEO's, shrinks, mediators, mediums, gurus, and astrologers negotiation is not a science.

Ronald Shapiro

Always...

> When you see a kid selling lemonade, buy some. Seeing that great big smile is worth the risk of permanently puckering your face if the sugar was left out.
>
> Robert Fulghum

Successful selling means helping people do what they do better.

Stephen Schiffman

Strategic alliances can lead to slow-motion acquisitions.

Rick Newton

Not to decide is to decide.

Harvey Cox

Charles Steinmetz (1865-1923) was a pioneering genius in harvesting electricity. After he retired, Steinmetz's former employers at General Electric occasionally relied on his brilliance.

Such was the case when an intricate set of machines broke down. In-house experts could not find the cause of this malfunction so GE leaders called Steinmetz.

After testing various parts, Steinmetz finally pinpointed the problem and marked the defective part with a piece of chalk. Steinmetz then submitted a bill for $10,000.

Surprised at this unexpected high price, GE honchos asked Steinmetz to resubmit an itemized statement. He complied with a new invoice that listed only two items:

<u>Invoice</u>

Making one chalk mark: $1.00
Knowing where to place it: $ 9,999.00

Unknown

The Money Paradox:

The sooner you ask for money, the less you get.

Seth Godin

Sales Presentations:

> Good format strengthens good content.
> Good content trumps bad format.
> Bad content is just bad.
>
> Gary A. Pokorn

In spite of the cost of living, it's still popular.

Kathleen Norris

In the sales business good logistics is no substitute for poor content; but poor logistics will kill good content almost every time.

Gary A. Pokorn

There were times when we lost money on every PC we sold, and so we were conflicted - if sales were down, was that bad news or good news?

Louis V. Gerstner, Jr.

Creditors have better memories than debtors.

Benjamin Franklin

At anything you choose to do, you'll be as good as the practice, drill, and rehearsal you go through before you actually perform the action.

Tom Hopkins

It has always seemed strange to me that selling - one of the most rewarding and important professions of all - isn't taught in any university. I know of no PhD's, Masters or Bachelors degrees awarded in Selling. You have to learn it on your own - a difficult journey at best.

Barry Trailer

You can no longer survive by interrupting strangers with a message they don't want to hear about a product they've never heard of, using methods that annoy them.

Seth Godin

Decide what you want, decide what you are willing to exchange for it. Establish your priorities and go for it.

H.L. Hunt

More and more these days I find myself pondering on how to reconcile my net income with my gross habits.

John Kirk Nelson

Sales Prospecting:

I will call a prospect for every reason I can possibly think of. The sun's up, the sun's down. It's been a good day, it's been a bad day. Just made a sale. Just lost a sale. Closed the deal; opened the deal. It doesn't matter.

Stephen Schiffman

You are not paid by the sale, you are paid by the contact. No contacts means no sales which means no earnings. Earnings are not started by sales, they are started by contacts.

Tom Hopkins

It's unwise to pay too much but it is worse to pay too little. When you pay too much, you lose a little money - that is all. When you pay too little, you sometimes lose everything, because the thing you bought was incapable of doing the thing it was bought to do. If you deal with the lowest bidder, it is well to add something for the risk you run. And if you do that, you will have enough to pay for something better.

John Ruskin

A bear who, displaying a $5 bill, had entered a bar and ordered a beer and; the owner of the bar directed the bartender to give the bear the beer, saying that since the bear didn't look very smart to only give it 25 cents in change. Having done as he had been instructed, and having watched incredulously as the bear placidly sipped the beer, the bartender finally could no longer contain himself and sought to engage the bear in conversation. "You know", he said to the bear, "we don't get many bears in this bar." To which the bear is said to have replied, "at $4.75 a beer, it's no wonder."

Norman R. Augustine

If you're selling drills, your prospects really couldn't care less about the drills. What they actually want are the holes.

Patrick Renvoise

When you're selling fire-extinguishers, open with the fire.

David Ogilvy

Let us never negotiate out of fear. But let us never fear to negotiate.

John F. Kennedy

The key to success is to raise your own energy. When you do, people will naturally be attracted to you. And when they show up, bill 'em.

Stuart Wilde

"Sales"

1. The top line of the income statement and the driving force of all organizations, ideas and progress. Also used to describe the greatest profession in history and greatest skill one can ever have.

Unknown

To a prospective customer evaluating vendor products or services, to quote a poker term, here's "What beats What":

- Better features beats lesser features
- An existing business relationship beats better features
- Saving money beats an existing business relationship
- Pain trumps all

Tony Marabotti

It seems that there was a pretzel stand in front of an office building in New York City. One day a man came out of the building, plunked down a quarter, and then went on his way without taking a pretzel. This happened every day for three weeks. Finally, the old lady running the stand spoke up, "Sir, excuse me. May I have a word with you?" The fellow answered, "I know what you're going to say. You're going to ask me why I give you a quarter every day and don't take a pretzel." The woman replied, "Not at all. I just wanted to tell you that the price is now 35 cents."

William Schreyer

<u>Book: VI Integrity-the Forever Journey</u>

Dedicated to the business professional who works for a Man-a-ger (man-i-gir) n 1. Coach, Teacher, instructor, Leader 2. Mr. Know-It-All, Ego With Legs 3. One who has or will have an ulcer 4. One who apologizes to subordinates for the stupid actions of superiors 5. One who apologizes to superiors for the actions of subordinates.

Not everyone can do this for a living.

Unknown

It takes but a flash to change.
It takes forever to maintain change.

Tom Peters

People don't like to take orders, they like to take part.

Michael Angelo Caruso

The measure of a man's real character is what he would do if he knew he would never be found out.

Charles Kingsley

The secret of managing is to keep the guys who hate you away from the guys who are undecided.

Casey Stengel

The more unpleasant the message, the more effort that should go into communicating it.

Unknown

The best leaders… almost without exception and at every level, are master users of stories and symbols.

Tom Peters

To err is human, to forgive is not company policy.

Unknown

The boss always scheduled the weekly staff meeting for 4:30 on Fridays. When one of the employees finally got up the nerve to ask why, she explained; "I'll tell you why - I've learned that's the only time when none of you seem to want to argue with me."

Unknown

Written reports have purpose only if read by the King.

Wess Roberts

At the top is the mission statement.
And it begat the strategy.
And the strategy begat the tactics.
And the tactics begat the objectives that begat the tasks
that begat the people in cubicles who no longer beget
children because they're working all weekend trying to
finish the !@#$-ing assignments they've been given to
serve the all-powerful mission statement.

Rick Levine

Circumstances should never alter principles.

Oscar Wilde

"EMPOWERMENT":

A term meant to give survivors of restructure the
illusion they have a role in the company's future.

Unknown

"EXECUTIVE" (high powered):

> A golfer who calls the office from a cell phone every five holes to make sure employees haven't left for the day.
>
> Martin A. Ragaway

I believe the real difference between success and failure in a corporation can very often be traced to the question of how well the organization brings out the great energies and talents of its people.

Thomas J. Watson

Over the years I've learned a lot about coaching staffs and one piece of advice I would pass on to a young coach or corporate executive or even a bank president is this; Don't make them in your image. Don't even try. My assistants don't look alike, think alike, or have the same personalities. And I sure don't want them all thinking the way I do. You don't strive for sameness, you strive for balance.

Paul "Bear" Bryant

See that you are not your own obstacle.

Elbert Hubbard

Work without defined boundaries is work that may never end. And if you don't clearly define expectations, you will get what you deserve, not what you need.

Robert C. Anderson

Here is the fundamental problem: people think of execution as the tactical side of business, something leaders delegate while they focus on the perceived bigger issues. Execution is not just tactics - it is a discipline and a system. It has to be built into a company's strategy, its goals, and its culture. And the leader of the organization must be deeply engaged in it.

Larry Bossidy

Executives who see their role in terms of tasks are easily frustrated by interruptions from employees; those who see their role in terms of people find deep fulfillment in opportunities to meet needs, to empower, and to help.

Stephen R. Covey

Be prepared to kill, revise, or evolve an idea, but never give up on the company.

Jim Collins

Q: How many executives does it take to change a light bulb?

A: Two. One to assure the staff that everything possible is being done, while the other tries to screw the bulb into a water faucet.

Paul Dickson

To add growth, lead followers - to multiply, lead leaders.

John C. Maxwell

If you always do what you always did, you'll always get what you always got.

Chris Coniglio

In a moment of decision, the best thing you can do is the right thing to do. The worst thing you can do is nothing.

Theodore Roosevelt

Visionary companies make some of their best moves by experimentation, and - quite literally - accident. Let's just try a lot of stuff and keep what works.

Jack Walsh

Encourage; don't nitpick. Let people run with an idea. Have good people, and leave them alone.

3M Phrase

Look, do you want to make a decision on this? Or do you just want us all to drive home tonight and feel bad about it?

John F. Akers

Good managers sustain optimism.

Joe Torre

Bad news for leaders:

There's been an alarming increase in the number of things you know nothing about.

Unknown

Change is the breakfast of champions. When Positive Change is absent, complacency takes over and failure is just around the corner.

David Cottrell

Preserve the core - stimulate progress.

Jim Collins

There may be times when we are powerless to prevent injustice, but there must never be a time when we fail to protest.

Elie Wiesel

There is a **Hierarchy of Systems** in your business - four distinct components:

The first is, How we do it here.
The second is, How we recruit, hire, and train people to do it here.
The third is, How we manage it here.
The fourth is, How we change it here.

Michael E. Gerber

One more word about your time:

If you're in a leadership position, how you spend your time has enormous symbolic value. It will communicate what's important or what isn't far more powerfully than all the speeches you can give. Strategic change doesn't just start at the top. It starts with your calendar.

Andy Grove

A good boss is always a blessing.

D. Michael Abrashoff

With a lot to lose from jumping full force into a new product that could fail, established players are likely to hold back. Failure damages the added value of their other products, especially if the new product is clearly identified in any way with their existing ones. For that reason, they may avoid using existing brand names. All of this uncertainty neutralizes what would otherwise be a major advantage to the established players.

Barry J. Nalebuff

Leadership is the capacity to translate vision into reality.

Walter Winchell

One of the primary principles of leadership is that you get what you reward.

David Cottrell

The purpose of a compensation system should not be to get the right behaviors from the wrong people, but to get the right people on the bus in the first place, and to keep them there.

Jim Collins

I only want people around me who can do the impossible.

Elizabeth Arden

People don't at first follow worthy causes. They follow worthy leaders who promote worthy causes.

John C. Maxwell

One of the best ways to strengthen our independent will is to make and keep promises.

Stephen R. Covey

Simply put, you can't change a company without changing its management. I'm not saying they have to pack up their desks and be replaced. I'm saying that they themselves, every one of them, needs to change to be more in tune with the mandates of the new environment. They need to adapt. If they can't or won't, however, they will need to be replaced.

Andy Grove

Demand the best from everyone, but remember that everyone's best will not be the same.

Frank Alsteiner

Labor to keep alive in your breast that little spark of celestial fire called conscience.

George Washington

You can employ men and hire hands to work for you, but you will have to win their hearts to have them work with you.

William J. H. Boetcker

The job of leadership today is not just to make money. It is to make meaning.

John Seely Brown

The job of a professional manager is not to like people. And whether one approves of people or of the way they do their work, their performance is the only thing that counts and indeed the only thing that the professional manager is permitted to pay attention to.

Alfred P. Sloan

Without integrity, you can never develop trust. Without trust, you will never develop people. Without developing people, you will never maintain a following. And without followers, you have no one to lead.

David Cottrell

Leadership is personal.

Louis V. Gerstner, Jr.

Leaders make things possible. Exceptional leaders make them inevitable.

Lance Morrow

To lead yourself, use your head; to lead others, use your heart.

John C. Maxwell

What, then, are the main lessons in <u>My Years with General Motors</u>, at least as I read Alfred Sloan's intentions? This is how I would paraphrase them:

- The first is that management is a profession and that the manager is - or should be - a professional.
- Like any other professional, a physician, for instance, or a lawyer, the professional manager has a client; the enterprise.

Peter F. Drucker

We will forget and forgive any judgment error that you make, but integrity mistakes are forever.

David Cottrell

Building character strength is like building physical strength. When the test comes, if you don't have it, no cosmetics can disguise the fact that it just isn't there.

Stephen R. Covey

You know what makes leadership? It is the ability to get men to do what they don't want to do, and like it.

Harry S. Truman

Running an organization is easy when you don't know how, but very difficult when you do.

Price Pritchett

The administrative processes are as essential to a business as breathing. If the basic operational processes of your business fail, your company fails.

Bill Gates

The key to being a successful skipper is to see the ship through the eyes of the crew.

D. Michael Abrashoff

As you work to build your organization, remember this:

- Personnel determine the potential of the organization.
- Relationships determine the morale of the organization.
- Structure determines the size of the organization.
- Vision determines the direction of the organization.
- Leadership determines the success of the organization.

John C. Maxwell

In fact, in the end, management doesn't change culture. Management invites the workforce itself to change the culture.

Louis V. Gerstner, Jr.

Integrity is the moment of choice.

Stephen R. Covey

Leadership is not charisma. It is not Public Relations. It is not showmanship. It is performance, consistent behavior, trustworthiness.

Peter F. Drucker

Call it a universal law… You are exactly as credible (as a sales manager) as (your sales rep) is with you… Recognize him for what he is - a mirror of you.

Barry Trailer

Without the ability to lead, execution (of the plan) is impossible.

Albert Lee

A king or someone with power may move a man. But the man's soul is the man's responsibility alone. When facing God, he cannot say, "Others made me do thus; or Virtue was not convenient at the time."

King Israel

People will not follow you unless they trust you and they cannot trust you if you don't talk straight to them.

Diane Tracy

I will induce others to serve me, because of my willingness to serve others. I will cause others to believe in me, because I will believe in them, and in myself.

Napoleon Hill

Business education without execution is just entertainment.

Unknown

Finally - and perhaps the most important lesson - the professional manager is a servant. Rank does not confer privilege. It does not give power. It imposes responsibility.

Peter F. Drucker

To find out why people are leaving I assumed that low pay would be the first reason, but in fact it was fifth. The top reason was not being treated with respect or dignity; second was being prevented from making an impact on the organization; third, not being listened to; and fourth, not being rewarded with more responsibility. Further research disclosed an unexpected parallel with civilian life.

D. Michael Abrashoff

I came to see, at my time at IBM, that culture isn't just one aspect of the game - it is the game.

Louis V. Gerstner, Jr.

"ex-e-cu-tion" (ek si kyoo shun), n. 1. The missing
link. 2. The main reason companies fall short of their
promises. 3. The gap between what a company's leaders
want to achieve and the ability of their organizations to
deliver it. 4. Not simply tactics, but a system of getting
things done through questioning, analysis, and follow-
through.

Larry Bossidy

The first responsibility of a leader is to define reality.
The last is to say, "Thank you."

Max De Pree

The best people want and demand timely, effective
feedback.

Diane Tracy

Resistance to change takes three main forms:

- Opposition based on misunderstanding or rational
  objections
- Fear of personal consequences; and
- Emotional distrust.

Robert Heller

Life is full of paradoxes and so is management:

- The more you focus on the needs of your people, the more needs of the job will get met.
- The less you play policeman, the more control of the work you will have.
- The less you remind people of your power, the more power you will have to get the job done.
- The more you help people feel good about themselves, the better they will feel about you.

Diane Tracy

Stanley Gault CEO of Rubbermaid:

He responds to the accusation of being a tyrant with the statement, "Yes, but I'm a sincere tyrant."

Stanley Gault

The moment you feel the need to tightly manage someone, you've made a hiring mistake. The best people don't need to be managed. Guided, thought-led, yes. But not tightly managed.

Jim Collins

If you delegate responsibility without the authority, you will after a period of time, be given back the responsibility.

Jerry L. Mills, CPA

The conventional definition of management is getting work done through people, but real management is developing people through work.

Agha Hasan Abedi

There is never a wrong time to do the right thing.

Unknown

The true test of character is not how much we know how to do, but how we behave when we don't know what to do.

John Holt

The more tranquil a man becomes, the greater his success, his influence, his power for good.

James Allen

My Lord, is it a true answer you would like, or merely an agreeable one?

Bruce Thorton

The sequence of emotions in the case of a strategic inflection point goes more as follows: denial, escape or diversion, and finally, acceptance and pertinent action.

Andy Grove

Getting yourself out of the way. Your job is to be the facilitator of the process, not the director of their destiny. As a manager you are merely a guide on the person's journey to self-discovery.

Diane Tracy

In most companies, however, individual managers don't have the luxury of surviving a string of trials and errors in pursuit of the strategy that works. Rightly or wrongly, individual managers in most organizations believe that they cannot fail: If they champion a project that fails because the initial marketing plan was wrong, it will constitute a blotch on their track record, blocking their rise through the organization.

Clayton M. Christensen

Why change when we are so successful? To give our customers and ourselves the very best of what will be needed tomorrow.

David S. Pottruck

Perhaps the greatest mistake I've seen executives make is to confuse expectations with inspection.

Louis V. Gerstner, Jr.

Business is founded on confidence; success on cooperation.

John Henry Patterson

Businessmen go down with their businesses because they like the old way so well they cannot bring themselves to change.

Henry Ford

The knock at the door tells the character of the visitor.

T.K.V. Desikachar

I believe in hard work. It keeps the wrinkles out of the mind and spirit.

Helena Rubinstein

Dignity does not consist of possessing honors, but in deserving them.

Aristotle

Keep in mind always the present you are constructing. It should be the future you want.

Alice Walker

Leadership strategy:

When you are presenting an idea and are outlining its benefits, if the person stops you and brings up an argument or shows resistance, let it ride. Don't respond for a moment. And even then, don't respond directly.

Too many people seem to be in a too big a hurry to answer questions and overcome resistances. Instead of making a case, we shift our focus and lose momentum by directly answering objections. We forget that we are there to give a coherent, complete presentation.

But maybe if we weren't in such hurry to answer the questions, our audience would find that the full presentation of facts covers the objections and the question would not come up again.

Of course, a time comes when you must handle the resistance, and handle it once and for all. But that time is always the second time, never the first.

John L. Beckley

Were there none who were discontented with what they have, the world would never reach for anything better.

Florence Nightingale

Big shots are only little shots who keep shooting.

Christopher Morley

Initially, when no available product satisfies the functionality requirements the market has, the basis of competition, or the criteria by which product choice is made, tends to be product FUNCTIONALITY. Once two or more products credibly satisfy the market's demand for functionality, customers tend to choose a product and vendor based on RELIABILITY. But when two or more vendors improve to the point that they more than satisfy the reliability demanded by the market, the basis of competition shifts to CONVENIENCE. Again, as long as the market demand for convenience exceeds what vendors are able to provide, customers choose products on this basis and reward vendors with premium prices. Finally, when multiple vendors offer a package of convenient products the basis of competition shifts to PRICE.

Clayton M. Christensen

The art of progress is to preserve order amid change and to preserve change amid order.

Alfred North Whitehead

A people unused to restraint must be led, they will not be drove.

George Washington

Each of us is an impregnable fortress that can be laid waste only from within.

Timothy J. Flynn

Punctuality is the politeness of kings.

Louis XVIII

If you're looking for a big opportunity, seek out a big problem.

Unknown

Great spirits have always encountered violent opposition from mediocre minds.

Albert Einstein

Creating an organizational context in which this effort can prosper will be crucial, because rational resource allocation processes in established companies consistently deny disruptive technologies the resources they need to survive, regardless of the commitment senior management may ostensibly have made to the program.

Clayton M. Christensen

<u>Book VII: Cowboy Up - You'll Get Through It</u>

Dedicated to the American Cowboy – may we all learn to be more like them.

Now, I'm no cowboy; but I know one.

Cowboys are quiet, polite - men of few words; comfortable just listening while others around them bark at the moon nonstop.

No, I'm no cowboy; but I've heard one.

Cowboys have a reserve of strength far and above the average person – physical strength to be sure; but also great emotional strength.

I'm definitely no cowboy; but I've seen one.

Cowboys have the ability to remain in control even while every living thing around them, man and beast, spooks in mortal fear.

True, I'm no cowboy; but I've been protected by one.

Cowboys remain focused even with adrenaline rushing through their veins when they're bull riding, or racing flat out, one-handed on horseback, to rope an escaping calf.

Yes, I'm no cowboy; but I've lived with one.

Cowboys are fearless especially at the age of 15 when they look down in the shoot and prepare to mount a bare back bucking bronco at their very first high school rodeo competition.

Absolutely, I'm no cowboy; but I've filmed one looking down that very shoot.

Cowboys always believe they can. The cowboy feels that sigh of relief when he's all twisted up in the dirt, having fallen off a stumbling horse and the rodeo announcer comes on the PA system and says, "Well folks, he'll have an option for a re-ride."

So, I'm no cowboy, but I've sat next to his Mother in the stands when we heard that Rodeo Announcer come over the P.A. System to say, "Well folks, he'll have an option for a re-ride." And as the announcer glanced down to the stands to see her reaction he quickly added, "But his Mother says NO!"

You see, I know a lot about cowboys. That's why I'm so sure I'm not one. No, I'm no cowboy, but my son Kevin is. And every day I try to be a little bit more like him.

Gary A. Pokorn

A mistake is an event, the full benefits of which has not yet been turned to your advantage.

Peter Senge

What would you attempt to do if you knew you could not fail?

Robert Schuller

Life is a terrific gym. Every situation is an opportunity to practice.

Sylvia Boorstein

Expect the best. Prepare for the worst. Capitalize on what comes.

Zig Ziglar

If things go wrong, don't go with them.

Roger Babson

If I believe I cannot do something, it makes me incapable of doing it. But when I believe I can, then I acquire the ability to do it, even if I did not have the ability in the beginning.

Mahatma Gandhi

Adversity clarifies commitment.

Gary A. Pokorn

Failure is the opportunity to begin again more intelligently.

Henry Ford

The champions aren't always the ones who have the medals.

Unknown

Difficulties are meant to rouse, not discourage. The human spirit grows strong by conflict.

William Ellery Channing

Success isn't permanent, and failure isn't fatal.

Mike Ditka

Just when you think you've graduated from the school of experience, someone thinks up a new course.

Mary H. Waldrip

Problems are the price of progress.

Charles Kettering

In a fight between you and the world, bet on the world.

Franz Kafka

Everything looks like a failure in the middle.

Price Pritchett

Failure is the greatest opportunity I have to know who I really am.

John Killinger

Cowboy secrets to life's success:

1. Don't let your head strap your hand to anything your butt can't ride.
2. Never corner anything meaner than you.

Unknown

I never see a failure as failure, but only as the opportunity to develop my sense of humor.

Tom Hopkins

Real courage is being scared to death and saddling up anyway.

James P. Owen

Pain nourishes courage. You can't be brave if you've only had wonderful things happen to you.

Mary Tyler Moore

People asked Edison, "How did you feel when you failed over a thousand times"? "I did not fail a thousand times. I learned a thousand ways that it wouldn't work."

Thomas Edison

When you're riding through hell… keep riding.

James P. Owen

I'm not a failure if I don't make it. I'm a success because I tried.

Unknown

Fall down seven times. Stand up eight.

Japanese Proverb

It's how you show up at the showdown that counts.

Homer Norton

Perseverance and spirit have done wonders in all ages.

George Washington

Life is tough. But it's tougher when you're stupid.

John Wayne

I am not judged by the number of times I fail, but by the number of times I succeed, and the number of times I succeed is in direct proportion to the number of times I can fail and keep on trying.

Tom Hopkins

You may have to fight a battle more than once to win it.

Margaret Thatcher

The occasion is piled high with difficulty, and we must rise with the occasion.

Abraham Lincoln

I love a man that can smile in trouble, that can gather strength from distress, and grow brave by reflection.

Thomas Paine

No Winter lasts forever, no Spring skips its turn.

Hal Borland

If it is possible, it is done; if impossible, it shall be done.

Charles Alexander de Calonne

If there is no struggle, there is no progress.

Frederick Douglas

It takes courage to know when you ought to be afraid.

James A. Michener

Courage doesn't always roar. Sometimes courage is the quiet voice at the end of the day saying, "I will try again tomorrow."

Mary Anne Radmacher

The fishermen know that the sea is dangerous and the storm terrible, but they have never found these dangers sufficient reason for remaining ashore.

Vincent van Gogh

"COURAGE":

The ability to move in the right direction in spite of fear.

Unknown

One man with courage makes a majority.

Andrew Jackson

Courage is a special kind of knowledge; the knowledge of how to fear what ought to be feared and how to not fear what ought not to be feared.

David Ben-Gurian

Time gives good advice.

Maltese Proverb

"COURAGE":

Courage is the price life extracts for granting peace.

Amelia Earhart

Did you ever see dishonest calluses on a man's hands?

Henry Ford

There cannot be a crisis next week. My schedule is already full.

Henry A. Kissinger

Confidence is an important element in business; it may on occasion make the difference between one man's success and another's failure.

Alfred P. Sloan Jr.

People often say that motivation doesn't last. Well, neither does bathing – that's why we recommend it daily.

Zig Ziglar

I try to take one day at a time, but sometimes several days attack me at once.

Ashleigh Brilliant

This is a world of struggle. Life is not easy.

Joe Newton

A vacation is what you take when you can no longer take what you've been taking.

Earl Wilson

If you find yourself in a hole, the first thing to do is stop digging.

Unknown

Honest criticism is hard to take, particularly from a relative, a friend, an acquaintance, or a stranger.

Franklin P. Jones

Among the chief worries of today's business executives is the large number of unemployed still on the payrolls.

Unknown

Patience is the best remedy for every trouble.

Plautus

"ADVERSITY":

Adversity has the effect of eliciting talents, which, in prosperous circumstances, would have lain dormant.

Horace

Being "Cautious" is never making the same mistake once.

Unknown

Life breaks us. And when we heal, we're stronger on the broken parts.

Ernest Hemingway

There can be constructive worry if it is directed towards positive goals.

Joe Newton

Brain researchers tell us that given ambiguity, the human mind always seems to decipher what it perceives as negative. The brain's system has been programmed to protect us, to amplify negative presumptions and minimize the positive. The higher you get in the organization, the more people notice you, and the greater the implications of your behavior.

David S. Pottruck

God's delays are not God's denials.

Robert H. Schuller

Will applied to any conflict creates energy.

Conflict without will creates frustration.

Conflict with will creates resolution.

Michael E. Gerber

Gentlemen, enlisted men may be entitled to morale problems, but officers are not.

General George C. Marshall

Worry is interest paid on trouble before it falls.

William Ralph Inge

That which we persist in doing becomes easier to do, not that the nature of the thing has changed, but that our ability to do has increased.

Emerson

If every day was a constant struggle, it usually meant I was going in the wrong direction.

Doug Peterson

Fatigue is often caused not by work but by worry, frustration, and resentment. We rarely get tired when we are doing something interesting and exciting.

Dale Carnegie

The key to success is tolerating boredom.

Robert K. Copper

God grant me the serenity to accept the things I cannot change; courage to change the things I can; and wisdom to know the difference.

Unknown

You may forget how you behaved when the going got tough, but others won't.

Mark Burnett

The single biggest danger in business and life, other than outright failure, is to be successful without being resolutely clear about why you are successful in the first place.

Robert Burgelman

Nothing in the world can take the place of persistence. Talent will not; nothing is more common than unsuccessful individuals with talent. Genius will not; unrewarded genius is almost a proverb. Education will not; the world is full of educated derelicts. Persistence and determination alone are omnipotent.

Calvin Coolidge

Tough times don't last;

tough people do.

Mike Shanahan

Everyone who got where he is had to begin where he was.

Robert Louis Stevenson

To the medieval mind the possibility of doubt did not exist.

William Manchester

It's wonderful what you can do when you have to.

C.S. Lewis

It is easy to dodge our responsibilities, but we cannot dodge the consequences of dodging our responsibilities.

Joseph Stamp

Always borrow from pessimists. They never expect to get it back.

Unknown

A bottomless cup of wake-up is a constant source of energy, inspiration, and optimism.

Tim Sanders

God created man because he enjoys stories.

Yiddish Proverb

The Cardinal Conundrum:

An optimist believes we live in the best of all possible worlds. A pessimist fears this is true.

Unknown

"Pessimist":

A person who not only expects the worst, but makes the most of it when it happens.

"Optimist":

The person who makes it possible for the pessimist to know how happy he or she isn't.

Unknown

I am convinced that life is 10% what happens to me and 90% how I react to it.

Charles Swindell

The pessimist may be right in the long run, but the optimist has a better time during the trip.

Unknown

"What does the optimist say about the glass and the water?" he asked. "It's half full", was the reply. "And what does the pessimist say?" he queried. "It's half empty." "And what does the process engineer have to say about it?" Silence - until the consultant revealed the new additional answer: "Looks like you've got twice as much glass as you need there."

Unknown

No sense in being pessimistic. It wouldn't work
anyway.

Unknown

The single most significant decision I can make on a
day-to-day basis is my choice of attitude.

Charles R. Swindell

Enthusiasm is not a random mood; it's a daily choice.

Joe Takash

Reflect upon your present blessings, of which every
man has many; not on your past misfortunes, of which
all men have some.

Charles Dickens

Smile:

> You get paid the same whether you are having a
> good time or not.

Frank Alsteiner

A pessimist is one who makes difficulties of his
opportunities; an optimist is one who makes
opportunities of his difficulties.

Reginald B. Mansell

A smile on someone else's face can make you feel good too – especially a cheerful expression on the face of your boss. Having a boss who is, as a habit, cheerful and pleasant, is one of the nicest things that can happen to you.

Likewise, developing a cheerful attitude is one of the nicest things you can do for the people who work for you. No latter how capable you are otherwise, a cheerful, friendly attitude will produce better results.

John L. Beckley

Few things are harder to put up with than the annoyance of a good example.

Mark Twain

Be happy today and everyday because you're dead a long time.

Johnny Unitas

Everything is always impossible before it works.

Hunt Greene

Whether the glass is half empty or half full depends on whether you're drinking or pouring.

Anthony Boxer

Hope is the feeling you have that the feeling you have isn't permanent.

Jean Kerr

Self-belief is a simple matter of focusing on what you do have.

Joe Takash

Every day that we wake up is a good day. Every breath that we take is filled with hope for a better day. Every word that we speak is a chance to change what is bad into something good.

Walter Mosley

Pessimists calculate the odds. **Optimists** believe they can overcome them.

Ted Koppel

Never regret. If it's good, it's wonderful. If it's bad, it's experience.

Victoria Holt

Unless you're thinking positively, you're thinking negatively.

Tom Hopkins

A co-worker bumped into me at the convenience store just as the sales clerk was telling me that I did not have a winning Power Ball lottery ticket. He asked me, "How's it going?" When I replied, "Great!" he said he was surprised. "But you just heard you lost the big lottery", expecting me to be more discouraged or at least a little disappointed. I simply explained, "I'm already rich, I just don't have a lot of money."

Gary A. Pokorn

Optimism is an intellectual choice.

Diana Schneider

Give young people a context where they can translate a positive imagination into reality.

Thomas L. Friedman

When nothing is sure, everything is possible.

Margaret Drabble

Stick with the optimists. It's going to be tough enough even if they're right.

James Reston

Retirement should be based on the tread, not the mileage.

Allen Ludden

Why not make the best of things? Any fool can make the worst of them.

Charles L. Bromley

If we did all the things we are capable of doing, we would literally astound ourselves.

Thomas Edison

Recall what has been said about the subconscious mind resembling a fertile garden spot, in which weeds will grow in abundance, if the seeds of more desirable crops are not sown therein.

Napoleon Hill

Why not go out on a limb? Isn't that where the fruit is?

Frank Scully

Every day is a leap of faith.

Lizz Wright

Confidence is courage at ease.

Daniel Maher

He who fears no truths has nothing to fear from lies.

Thomas Jefferson

The great thing about tomorrow? I can be better tomorrow than I am today.

Tiger Woods

A prudent person profits from personal experience, a wise one from the experiences of others.

Joseph Collins

Both men arrived at the Knox College campus by carriage and walked into the college's impressive new building that later came to be called *Old Main*. The debate was held on the east side of the building. As the two men, along with other dignitaries, stepped through a window on to the stage it is reported that Lincoln said, "Well, at last I have gone through college."

Owen Muelder

I'm not happy, I'm cheerful. There's a difference. A happy woman has no cares at all. A cheerful woman has cares but has learned how to deal with them.

Beverly Sills

If you can find a path with no obstacles, it probably doesn't lead anywhere.

Frank A. Clark

Don't let what you cannot do interfere with what you can do.

John Wooden

The secret of patience:

Do something else in the meantime.

Unknown

Pain is inevitable. Suffering is optional.

Adlai E. Stevenson

Dare to be naïve.

R. Buckminster Fuller

Worry about being better; bigger will take care of itself.

Gary Comer

One step in the right direction, if continued, leads away from the paths of destruction.

Joseph Bruchac

Sometimes I confuse being serious about what I do with taking myself too seriously.

Tom Connellan

My rule is always to do the business of the day in the day.

Wellesley Wellington

When you're on a roll, keep rolling!

Steve Whitehead

Just because things are not going perfectly does not mean they are not going well.

Al Groh

Smooth seas do not make skillful sailors.

African proverb

Avoiding danger is no safer in the long run than outright exposure. The fearful are caught as often as the bold.

Helen Keller

The credit belongs to the man who is actually in the arena, whose face is marred by dust and sweat and blood; who strives valiantly; who errs, and comes short again and again, because there is no effort without error and shortcoming.

Teddy Roosevelt

For myself I am an optimist – it does not seem to be much use being anything else.

Winston Churchill

It takes the sun to create a shadow – accept that the dark and the light live side by side in all of us.

Chellie Campbell

What would life be if we had no courage to attempt anything?

Vincent van Gogh

You're blessed when you're content with just who you are – no more, no less. That's the moment you find yourselves proud owners of everything that can't be bought.

Matthew 5: Verse 4

<u>Book VIII: Talk Less. Say More</u>

Dedicated to Irv Kupcinet who was an American newspaper columnist for the Chicago Sun-Times and a broadcast personality based in Chicago, Illinois. In 1952, "Kup" became a pioneer in the television talk show genre when he landed his own talk show where he coined the phrase, "The Art of Conversation". And to the professionals today whose tools of their trade are the words they use in business. And finally, to everyone who has the ability to say what they mean; and mean what they say.

Not everyone can do this for a living.

Gary A. Pokorn

Have a take, don't suck, or you'll get run.

Jim Rome

Sometimes you have to be silent in order to be heard.

Unknown

Subtlety is saying what you think, but then leaving before anyone really understands what you meant.

> Unknown

A simple, elegant solution can be understood, developed, and implemented. With each complicating factor, the probability of success diminishes exponentially.

> Daniel T. Scott

If you can't convince them, confuse them.

> Harry S. Truman

Left hand, right hand, it doesn't matter. I'm amphibious.

> Charles Shackleford

Blessed is the man who, having nothing to say, abstains from giving us wordy evidence of the fact.

> Elliot

"DEJA MOO":

The feeling you've heard this bull before.

> Unknown

I do not object to people looking at their watches when I am speaking, but I strongly object when they start shaking them to make sure they are still working.

Lord Birkett

You will be happier if you will give people a bit of your heart rather than a piece of your mind.

Unknown

The art of translation lies less in knowing the other language than in knowing your own.

Ned Rorem

If a thing goes without saying, let it.

Unknown

"Extinction":

The absence of feedback can cause people to withdraw their commitment.

Tom Connellan

What this country needs is more free speech worth listening to.

Lawrence J. Peter

"GYST":

Don't write anything until you "Get Your Stuff Together." Lots of gas-filled balloons are launched from word processors by people who began to write before they really knew what they were talking about, why they were talking about it, or to whom they were talking.

Tom Sant

My sources may be unreliable, but their information is fascinating.

Unknown

Courtor's Rule:

If people listened to themselves more often, they would talk less.

Unknown

Study the words, no doubt, but look behind them to the thought they indicate, and having found it, throw the words away as the chaff when you have sifted out the grain.

Hindu Proverb

To say nothing frequently reflects an admirable command of language.

Unknown

I've spoken my mind even when I knew that what I said might be unpopular, because I believe that to speak your mind is essential, to take part in controversy is important.

Lilli Palmer

Nothing is so simple that it can't be misunderstood.

Junior Teague

A wise chieftain never kills the Hun bearing bad news. Rather, the wise chieftain kills the Hun who fails to deliver bad news.

Wess Roberts

We hear only half of what is said to us, understand only half of that, believe only half of that, and remember only half of that.

Mignon McLaughlin

The most frequent observable act of a leader is communication.

David S. Pottruck

Sometimes I get an e-mail that begins, "In keeping with the dictum that bad news should travel faster than good news, here's a gem."

Bill Gates

Nothing is quite so annoying as to have someone go right on talking when you're trying to interrupt.

Unknown

When faced with an objection:

- Try the re-statement technique; "Can you restate that?"
- Or use the show-me-how technique; "Can you show me how that would work?"

Unknown

All things being equal, a short, clear proposal is more persuasive than a long, densely worded one. Because your proposal is brief, it's more likely to be read first. That's to your advantage, because it means that your offering establishes the baseline against which others are judged. Because your proposal is easy to understand – because it's readable – it will seem more logical than other proposals.

Tom Sant

He who graduates today, and stops learning tomorrow, is uneducated the day after.

Newton D. Baker

When there's nothing more to say, don't be sayin' it.

James P. Owen

Short words are the best words, and old words, when they are short, are the best words of all.

Winston Churchill

The mistakes we make being nice yield only small penalties.

Unknown

The purpose of an education is to replace an empty mind with an open one.

Malcolm Forbes

I apologize for writing such a long letter. I didn't have the time to write you a short one.

Pascal

He can compress the most words into the smallest ideas of any man I ever met.

Abraham Lincoln

A closed mouth gathers no feet.

Unknown

Natural, human conversation is the true language of commerce.

Seth Godin

Only speak when your words are better than your silence.

Unknown

Listening is the most potent talent of a leader, especially to what may be unsaid.

Cal Turner, Jr.

Be who you are and say what you feel 'cause people who mind don't matter and people who matter don't mind.

Theodor Seuss Geisel

"Feedback":

> It truly is the lunch of champions.
>
> > Stephen R. Covey

"Diplomacy", n.

> The patriotic act of lying for one's country.
>
> > Ambrose Bierce

The best audience is intelligent, well-educated and a little drunk.

> Alben W. Barkley

Use short sentences. A sentence is an idea. Sentences work best when they contain only one idea. And they work even better when they're short and simple. Try to keep your average sentence length to between seventeen and twenty words.

> Tom Sant

The hallmark of the truly selfish man is the man who will not listen to anyone.

> Humphrey Carpenter

The sweetest of all sounds is praise.

Xenophon

The real art of conversation is not only to say the right thing in the right place but to leave unsaid the wrong thing at the tempting moment.

Dorothy Neville

When you talk, you repeat what you already know. When you listen, you often learn something.

Jared Sparks

The most motivating thing one person can do for another is to listen.

Roy Moody

Coaching is not telling people what to do. When you tell somebody something, regardless of how brilliant it is, it is like a flicker of light passing through his gray matter. When people discover something for themselves it is like a brilliant light bulb that goes off in their heads.

Diane Tracy

Each employee has to asked: "What should we hold <u>you</u> accountable for? What information do <u>you</u> need? And, in turn, What information do <u>you</u> owe the rest of us?"

Peter Drucker

The phrase, "I have good news and I have bad news", is really just bad news. We know this because we learn of good news this way; "You're not going to freaking believe this, but…"

Gary A. Pokorn

In the cowboy's mind, the bigger the mouth, the better it looks shut.

James P. Owen

A gossip is one who talks to you about others; a bore is one who talks to you about himself; and a brilliant conversationalist is one who talks to you about yourself.

Lisa Kirk

Many attempts to communicate are nullified by saying too much.

Robert K. Greenleaf

If I am to speak for ten minutes, I need a week for preparation; if fifteen minutes, three days; if half an hour, two days; if an hour, I am ready now.

Woodrow Wilson

Veterinarian's Office sign:

All unattended children will be given a free kitten.

Unknown

The best way to learn is the simplest:
1. Analyze the task to be learned
2. Set the climate for learning
3. Tell the learners how to do the task
4. Show the learners how to do the task
5. Let the learners do the task themselves
6. Review their work in ways that reinforce their achievements and set goals for improvement

Geri McArdle

Good teaching is one-fourth preparation and three-fourths theatre.

Gail Godwin

Give your proposal a title. Remember that the title of your proposal may be the first part of it that clients read. Avoid generic titles.

A good title should do the following:

- Describe your recommendation
- Contain an active verb that stresses a benefit to the client
- Focus on results, not product names
- Avoid any use of jargon

Tom Sant

Blessed are those who can give without remembering and take without forgetting.

Elizabeth Bibesco

We all need feedback. I receive it regularly from my boss and others and if I don't get it I ask for it, because I need that information in order to know what to do differently – so that I am always clear on what is expected of me.

Unknown

When the circus comes to town, go see it. It's the circus – does everything need explaining?

Robert Fulghum

To prepare for a decrease in time:

Make notes to yourself on the outline you already have. Mark the support material you will keep in the body if your time is cut to 75 percent. Then put another mark by the material you will keep if time is cut by 50 percent.

Geri McArdle

In the text below, identify (inspect) the number of f's that appear:

```
Finished files are the result
of years of scientific study
combined with the experience
of years.
```

(Answer – 6)

George Eckes

The trouble with practical jokes is that very often they get elected.

Will Rogers

I am neither so green that I cannot teach; nor am I so gray that I cannot learn.

Gary A. Pokorn

Creativity begins with imitation. Michelangelo learned his techniques by imitating – that is, by studying – the methods of others before he began creating his own masterpieces.

Unknown

Make the most of the best and the least of the worst.

Robert Louis Stevenson

Establishing goals is all right if you don't let them deprive you of interesting detours.

Doug Larson

When you teach people, you let them know that they are worth investing time in which helps to win their trust.

Unknown

Between two evils, choose neither; between two goods, choose both.

Tyron Edwards

In America today, you can be anything you want to be; and most people are.

Gary A. Pokorn

Empowering means defining the parameters in which people are allowed to operate, and then setting them free.

D. Michael Abrashoff

There are only as many days in the year as you make use of. One man gets only a week's value out of a year while another man gets a full year's value out of a week.

Charles Richards

Partnership means, "Let's you and I agree to do things my way."

Naomi R. Blakeslee

Somewhat analogous to the cross-eyed discuss thrower; he seldom came out ahead, but he sure does keep the crowd alert.

Irving Bluestone

Truth exists; only falsehood has to be invented.

Georges Braque

Principles are the simplicity on the far side of complexity.

Stephen R. Covey

Golfer Tommy Bolt is known for his sweet swing and foul temper. While giving a clinic to a group of amateurs, Bolt tried to show his softer side by involving his 14-year old son in the lesson. "Show the nice folks what I taught you", said Bolt. His son obediently took a 9-iron, cursed, and hurled it into the sky.

Thomas Roswell

All I've ever wanted was an honest, week's pay for an honest day's work.

Sergeant Bilko

"Timing":

I just heard the sad story of the comic who lost his timing. He stepped on his own lines, tried to talk over the laughs, and lost his ability to build a strong close. He got fired from one gig after another until he got so depressed, he decided to end it all. He went down to the railroad tracks and threw himself behind a train.

The Jokesmith

The difference between being an elder statesman and posing successfully as an elder statesman is practically negligible.

T.S. Eliot

When Elizabeth Dole was appointed Secretary of
Transportation by President Reagan in 1985, magazines
covered the Dole marriage – she as cabinet member, he
as powerful senator. After a photo ran that showed
them making up their bed in their apartment, a man
wrote a complaining letter to Bob Dole, praising
Elizabeth's skills but adding, "You've got to stop doing
the work around the house. You're causing problems
for men across the country. You don't know the half of
it", Dole wrote back. "The only reason she was helping
was because they were taking pictures."

Clifton Fadiman

The incident of an undersized lawyer in an acrimonious
stump debate with the massive Robert Toombs. Toombs
called out, "Why, I could button your ears back and
swallow you whole." The little fellow retorted, "and if
you did, you would have more brains in your stomach
than you ever had in your head."

Abraham Lincoln

Never mistake knowledge for wisdom. One helps you
make a living and the other helps you make a life.

Sandra Carey

Nothing makes me more tolerant of a neighbor's noisy party than being there.

Franklin P. Adams

There are times in our lives when imbalance is balance, when a short-term focus contributes to our overall mission in life.

Stephen R. Covey

During the final seconds of an especially tense game, Boston Celtics coach K.C. Jones called a time-out. As he gathered the players together at courtside, he diagrammed a play, only to have Larry Bird say, "Get the ball out to me and get everyone out of my way." Jones responded, "I'm the coach, and I'll call the plays!" Then he said, "Get the ball to Larry and get out of his way." It just shows that when the real leader speaks, people listen.

John C. Maxwell

A man begins cutting his wisdom teeth the first time he bites off more than he can chew.

Herb Caen

A wife invited some people to dinner. At the table, she turned to their six-year-old daughter and said, "Would you like to say the blessing? I wouldn't know what to say", the girl replied. "Just say what you hear Mommy say", the wife answered. The daughter bowed her head and said, "Lord, why on earth did I invite all these people to dinner?"

Unknown

From the Department of Darned Good Ideas...

Peter Drucker

If you want to live like a Republican, vote like a Democrat – take good care of the losers and left-behinds.

Thomas L. Friedman

A story is told of a Woman Member of Parliament who, after an extensive tirade at a social function, scornfully told the Prime Minister, "Mr. Churchill, you are drunk", to which Churchill replied, "And you Madam, are ugly. But I shall be sober tomorrow."

Winston Churchill

Patience is something you admire in the driver behind you, but not in the one ahead.

Bill McGlashen

Cooperation is doing with a smile what you have to do anyway.

Unknown

We hope that when the insects take over the world they will remember with gratitude how we took them along on all our picnics.

Bill Vaughan

Nothing is so simple that it cannot be misunderstood.

Gypsey Teague

The supreme purpose of history is a better world.

Herbert Hoover

The most valuable of all talents... that of never using two words when one will do.

Thomas Jefferson

May I forget what ought to be forgotten; and recall, unfailing, all that ought to be recalled, each kindly thing, forgetting what might sting.

Mary Carolyn Davies

Everybody's got to believe in something. I believe I'll have another beer.

W.C. Fields

Book IX: Playing to Win

Dedicated to Joe Newton…

Playing to _**win**_
like Joe Newton

Everyone has a hero; Joe Newton is one of mine.

Who is Joe Newton anyway? Well, he is one of the most successful high school coaches in America. More importantly, how he coached his teams to compete has a direct, cross-over application to our everyday lives.

York Community High School Elmhurst, Illinois. I grew up in Elmhurst, a town of about 50,000 residents. Elmhurst is a near western suburb of Chicago and York High School is the one public high school in Elmhurst. My brother graduated from York in 1962; I followed, graduating in 1971.

Joe Newton was my brother's track coach in 1960 & '61, that's how I first became acquainted with "Tiger Joe". Coach Newton became a life long influence for me starting during my years at York - even though I was never a member of any of his teams. Now that's some kind of influence.

In addition to being the York varsity boys' track & field coach, Joe Newton was also the varsity boys' cross country coach for a period spanning more than 40 years.

During that span, he became one of the most successful boys' high school cross country coaches in the nation. I've summarized the competitive performance of Coach Newton's teams from 1961 to 2000; 40 seasons. It would be very difficult to find any other coach that has accomplished what he did.

Because of his extraordinary success, I've tried to pattern my approach to business on his competitive principles. We would all like to enjoy competitive success similar to Joe Newton's. Before we look York's cross country results, let me share a little more background to help explain why I'm insisting that his success is unique and thus worthy of sharing this story with you.

In Elmhurst, in order to attend York High School a student's parents or guardian had to be an Elmhurst resident. What this "residency rule" meant is Coach Newton had no opportunity to recruit his cross country athletes. He simply watched and waited as the community's junior high schools "fed" incoming freshman boys into York. There was even a level of "competition" for these freshmen from two local parochial high schools. However, the important background point I'm emphasizing here is that Joe Newton's success was <u>not</u> based on his ability to recruit superior athletes into his program.

Like every 4-year high school, Joe Newton's teams turned over approximately 25% of their athletes every year; 100% every 4 years, through graduation. Every high school coach has to face the reality of this turnover – that makes Joe Newton's consistency of success for over 4 decades even more remarkable.

During the period from 1961 to 2000, running on the cross country team was not generally the top choice for incoming freshmen boys. High school sports at that time attracted the strongest and most capable athletes to the football team first; with the soccer team generally preferred second. Running cross country was definitely not considered much of a "glamour sport".

Let me recap:

- No recruiting of talent – he "played" with whoever came out for his teams.
- A minimum 25% turnover of his team every year (through graduation).
- An absolute 100% turnover of his team every 4 years.
- 40 years of continuous success – locally, statewide, and nationally.

Adding another dimension to the mystery of his success, he did not keep his coaching methods a secret. Joe Newton's first book, The Long Green Line, was published in 1969. It was a book detailing the success of York's cross country teams since his arrival. Coach Newton published two more books; Motivation is the Name of the Game; and Running to the Top soon thereafter. Now these weren't biographies or books on theory. He wrote about how to coach high school boys cross country. He wrote about execution. In one of his books, he even detailed his day-by-day practice schedules; diet plans; time "splits"; the works!

This meant that literally every other high school coach could read <u>exactly</u> how Joe Newton approached coaching his teams. In theory, competing coaches could "mirror" York's program improving their odds of winning. In theory, if they happen to have a superior class of athletes during the 40 year period in question, their high school program could have been the dominant program over York's. In theory.
Okay, let's take a look at his numbers for the period of 1961-2000 (40 seasons of competition):

- Dual meet **winning percentage** (York vs. one opponent) York won **94%** of these meets
- Conference **championships** (York vs. 8-10 other high schools) York won **37 out of 40 years**
- State of Illinois race performance (York vs. <u>all</u> high school teams in Illinois)- York's results;

> **State championships**
> **21 out of 40 years**
> State **runner-up**
> **10 out of 40 years**
> Total **Top 5** finishes
> **37 out of 40 years**
> Total **Top 10** finishes
> **39 out of 40 years**

(Remember; 25% turnover every year; 100% turnover every 4 years.)

♦ National competition* - York's results

> **National championships
   20 out of 40 years**
> Total **Top 3** finishes
   33 out of 40 years

* As recorded by the "Cross Country US Postal" organization and including more than 10,100 high schools throughout the USA; with 25% turnover every year...

I think you'll agree Joe Newton's teams **play to _win_** – win every time; win every day; win every year; win at every level of competition, for more than 40 straight years. How would you like that level of competitive success in your business? I know I would.

In the 1970's, when I became a fan of Joe Newton's teams, I didn't know very much about cross country running. I thought as a long distance runner, you just ran; a lot. (Something I did not want to do myself.) For all I knew at the time, Coach Newton could have been putting lifts in his teams' shoes to trick them into thinking they were always running downhill.

Seriously, it didn't take too much to figure out that it wasn't luck, or chance (or lifts), or recruiting, or "magic" or any other secrets that were behind York's extraordinary success. No, Joe Newton was truly doing something different than his competition to win (and win and win...). So I read his books; I chatted with him frequently; and I learned. Let me summarize a few of the lessons learned.

In playing to win, Joe Newton had perfected the principles of structured process + continuous improvement + dedication to practice + motivation through recognition + fun! (And believe me, there's no better way to have fun than by winning.) He put all of these principles together and then committed himself and his runners to the application of these principles every day for more than 40 years.

One of the outcomes of his commitment was that his teams beat their dual meet competitors 94 times of out every 100 races year-in and year-out for more than 40 years!

If Joe could do it with teenaged boys, what do you think we could in our daily lives? After all, if we're going to work for a living, we might as well **play to _win_**. Yes?

Gary A. Pokorn

If better is even possible, good is not enough.

Joe Newton

But I firmly believe that any man's finest hour - his greatest fulfillment to all he holds dear - is that moment when he has worked his heart out in a good cause and lies exhausted on the field of battle - victorious.

Vince Lombardi

Luck is when preparation meets opportunity.

Joe Newton

The right people will do the right things and deliver the best results they're capable of, regardless of the incentive system.

Jim Collins

Never change a winning game; always change a losing one.

Bill Tilden

It is very easy to be ordinary but it takes courage to excel…

Joe Newton

"PACE"...

Notice that in the mile we do not allow for much of a slowing down of the pace in the third quarter. We certainly realize that at this point in the race there is great difficulty in maintaining the tempo and many coaches feel this is the proper time to rest. We feel it is essential to maintain the pace at this time and that quite often the slowing down is merely a psychological thing.

Joe Newton

It requires a strong constitution to withstand repeated attacks of prosperity.

Joe Newton

Many enemies mean much honor...

Lilli Palmer

Burning desire... It eliminates the plodders, the wanters and the wishful thinkers.

Joe Newton

When you go through hurt, you achieve power.

Joe Newton

Glory is fleeting, but obscurity is forever.

Napoleon Bonaparte

Our competition got me out of bed in the morning; paranoia is a wonderful motivator.

Scott Deeter

"DISCIPLINE":

The ability to do what you don't want to do to become the person you want to become.

Unknown

I didn't come here to be told that I'm burning the candle at both ends, complained the patient to his doctor. I came for more wax.

Unknown

Former NBA center and coach Johnny Kerr said his biggest test as a coach came when he coached the then-expansion team the Chicago Bulls and his biggest player was 6'8" Erwin Mueller.

We had lost seven in a row and I decided to give a psychological pep talk before a game with the Celtics, Kerr said. I told Bob Boozer to go out and pretend he was the best scorer in basketball. I told Jerry Sloan to pretend he was the best defensive guard. I told Guy Rodgers to pretend he could run an offense better than any other guard, and I told Erwin Mueller to pretend he was the best rebounding, shot-blocking, scoring center in the game. We lost the game by 17.

I was pacing around the locker room afterward trying to figure out what to say when Mueller walked up, put his arm around me, and said, "Don't worry about it Coach. Just pretend we won."

James S. Hewett

Big Hairy Audacious Goal:

It has a clear finish line, so the organization can know when it has achieved the goal; people like to shoot for finish lines.

Jim Collins

Talk to your enemies because they will tell you your faults.

Unknown

When rungs were missing, I learned to jump.

William Warfield

It's hard to bet a person who never gives up.

Babe Ruth

An advantage unused is a disadvantage.

Dave Weinbaum

A golfer, searching for a ball lost deep in the rough, asked the caddie, "Why do you keep looking at that pocket watch? It isn't a watch", the caddie said. "It's a compass."

Unknown

Circumstances? What are circumstances? I make circumstances.

Napoleon Bonaparte

The breakfast of champions is not cereal. It's the opposition.

Nick Seitz

It is not enough that we win – all others must lose.

Genghis Khan

In business, cannibalize yourself rather than let someone else eat you alive.

Barry J. Nalebuff

The most valuable thing you can ever own is your image of yourself as a winner in the great game of life, as a contributor to the betterment of humankind, as an achiever of worthy goals.

Tom Hopkins

Everyone dreams. Some people are just more active participants.

Unknown

Reach for the heavens and hope for the future and all that we can be not just what we are.

John Denver

Strive relentlessly to improve what we do and how we do it.

David S. Pottruck

Let your imagination put you in a grandstand at the Seattle version of the Special Olympics. There are nine contestants, all physically or mentally disabled, assembled at the starting line for the 100-yard dash. At the gun, they all start out, not exactly in a dash, but with relish to run the race to the finish and win. All, that is, except one boy who stumbles on the asphalt, tumbles over a couple of times, and begins to cry. The other eight hear the boy cry. They slow down and look back. They all turn around and go back... every one of them. As you watch, one girl with Down's Syndrome bends down and kisses him. You hear her say, "This will make it better." All nine link arms and walk across the finish line together. Everyone in the stadium, including you, stands up, and the cheering goes on for several minutes. People who were actually there are still telling the story, fours years later. Why? Because deep down we know this one thing: What matters in this life is helping others win, even if it means changing our own course.

David S. Pottruck

Coaching is for everybody, every day.

Linda Richardson

Only the mediocre are always at their best.

Jean Giraudoux

There's only one thing worse than somebody who quits and leaves – and that's somebody who quits and stays.

Kevin Davis

Character consists of what you do on the third and fourth tries.

James A. Michener

If there exists no possibility of failure, then victory is meaningless.

Robert H. Schuller

Who stands to gain if you become a player in a game? Who stands to lose?

Barry J. Nalebuff

I've been up against tough competition all my life. I wouldn't know how to get along without it.

Walt Disney

Al McGuire, former head basketball coach of Marquette University, once said, "A team should be an extension of the coach's personality. My teams were arrogant and obnoxious."

Al McGuire

If you don't know what you want, you won't recognize it when you get it.

Unknown

A few meanings:

- When you lose, don't lose the lesson.
- Learn the rules so you know how to break them properly.
- Live a good, honorable life. Then when you're older, you'll be able to enjoy it a second time.
- Judge your success by what you had to give up in order to get it.

Unknown

The biggest opportunities – and the biggest profits – don't come from playing the game differently. They come from changing the game itself.

Barry J. Nalebuff

All of the great companies in the world out-execute their competition day in and day out.

Price Pritchett

I handle lots of losses and defeats without losing confidence because I know I'm a winner.

Tom Hopkins

The defender is at an inherent disadvantage. He may not even know he is being attacked until the attack is well along.

Richard Foster

Motivation is what gets you started. Habit is what keeps you going.

Jim Ryun

Victory goes to the player who makes the next-to-last mistake.

Savielly Grigoryvitch Tartakower

When an archer misses the mark, he turns and looks for the fault within. Failure to hit the bull's-eye is never the fault of the target. To improve your aim – improve yourself.

Gilbert Arland

How you do anything is how you do everything.

T. Harv Eker

Pain is temporary. Quitting lasts forever.

Lance Armstrong

Winning isn't getting ahead of others. It's getting ahead of yourself.

Roger Staubach

Every morning in Africa, a gazelle wakes up. It knows it must run faster than the fastest lion or it will be killed. Every morning a lion wakes up. It knows it must outrun the slowest gazelle or it will starve. It doesn't matter whether you are a lion or a gazelle. When the sun comes up, you better start running.

African proverb

Who wants a dream that's near-fetched?

Howard Schultz

Difficulty is the excuse history never accepts.

Edward R. Murrow

You can measure a man by the opposition it takes to discourage him.

Robert C. Savage

Drive like you stole it!

Unknown

Mediocre people have an answer for everything and are astonished at nothing.

Eugene Delacroix

To play it safe is not to play.

Robert Altman

Most people go to where the puck is; I go to where I think the puck will be.

Wayne Gretzky

Duty is a matter of the mind. **Commitment** is a matter of the heart.

Unknown

Good motivation is brought about by the intelligent application of positive reinforcement.

Joe Newton

Freedom means choosing your burden.

Hephzibah Menuhin

Only through curiosity can we discover opportunities and only by gambling can we take advantage of them.

Clarence Birdseye

Vision without effort is day dreaming; effort without vision is drudgery.

Unknown

Perpetual optimism is a force multiplier.

Colin Powell

Half the failures of this world in life arise from pulling in one's horse as he is leaping.

Julius and Augustus Hare

No abilities, however splendid, can command success without intense labor and persevering application.

Alexander T. Stewart

The big rewards come to those who travel the second, undemanded mile.

Bruce Barton

Be not afraid of greatness: some are born great, some achieve greatness, and some have greatness thrust upon them.

William Shakespeare

If you think you are beaten, you are,
    If you think you dare not, you don't.
        If you like to win, but you think you can't,
            It is almost certain you won't.

If you think you'll lose, you're lost,
    For out in the world we find,
        Success begins with a fellow's will –
            It's all in the state of mind.

If you think you are outclassed, you are,
    You've got to think high to rise,
        You've got to be sure of yourself before
            You can ever win a prize.

Life's battles don't always go
    To the stronger or faster man,
        But soon or late that man who wins
            Is the man who thinks he can.

Unknown

There is both peace and power in knowing and understanding who you are, where you're from and where you're going.

Doug Burgum

2nd Intermission

Afraid of flying

Preface:

You are a trusted advisor. You are about to be consulted. Please read the setting that follows and then prepare your recommendation either by selecting one of the multiple choice options or coming up with one your own.

Setting:

Jeana is an Employee Management Services sales producer, based in Seattle, Washington. Her career has progressed very nicely over the past 11 years. She has made a very good living and has had excellent results with an investment portfolio that has been professionally managed by her financial advisor. In the past 3 years Jeana has also made money by investing in $600,000-800,000 "spec" homes with two of her colleagues. Her brother is the builder and they just closed on the sale of their 7th house.

In addition to her sales and financial success, Jeana enjoys pursuing her personal "gift" of singing and acting and has performed semi-professionally in 2 or 3 seasonal productions over the past few years. She takes voice and language coaching along with music lessons every week and has done so since she was in high school. Although she is successful in her job and with her financial investments, her "life's passion" is her singing. She has never pursued this "passion" full-time, fearing failure. However, she knows she has the talent and continues to hold out hope that an opportunity will somehow surface in the future.

Jeana has retained an agent/attorney to manage and promote her singing and acting interests. Her agent is an expert in finding and promoting "new talent" and he's very enthusiastic about Jeana's possibilities. Unbeknownst to Jeana, her agent has been exploring the idea of an off-Broadway role as a way to break into the higher echelons of the profession. Although he has not spoken specifically to her about this idea, when he has asked generally about future direction, Jeana has stated that she is open to the possibilities of taking a leave-of-absence or even making a career change if the right opportunity came up. She has worked very hard in her sales profession and has been very successful. Financially, she can afford to pursue other interests for a year or two; even if it didn't work out she could always return to sales. Jeana has visited New York City many times and would be very comfortable with a cross-country relocation; for the right opportunity.

It is very early Thursday morning and Jeana's agent just called with great news. He has secured an audition for a part in an off-Broadway musical that is a perfect fit for Jeana's talents! The audition is scheduled for tomorrow afternoon at 4:00pm Eastern Time in New York. Jeana's agent has already booked her on a late flight from Seattle/Tacoma Airport to New York's LaGuardia along with limo service from the airport in New York to the Marriott Marquis Hotel on 42nd and Broadway; just a short distance from the theater. Jeana can fly out tonight, rest up tomorrow morning, and then walk a few blocks to her audition; perfectly orchestrated by her agent.

Here's the dilemma: Jeana is deathly afraid of flying.

In a panic, Jeana has just called you for advice. She would like your help on deciding which of the possibilities she has worked out in her mind would be best; and she is also open to any other suggestions you might have.

As her trusted advisor, what option would you recommend?

Option A: Jeana should call the Producer and explain that she has a family crisis that will prevent her from being in New York tomorrow (i.e. Friday) afternoon. However, she is confident that she can resolve the matter and still be in New York first thing Monday morning. Assuming the Producer agrees with a slight rescheduling of the audition, Jeana plans to hire a private transportation company to drive her to New York in a modestly-sized RV so she can sleep and eat during the round-the-clock drive across the country. That way she will show up Monday morning refreshed and ready for the audition. Although this private transportation service is a bit expensive, when she deducts the cost of the flight, limo and hotel, she has decided she can well afford the incremental cost to avoid her flying phobia. The primary drawback to this idea is the risk of the Producer selecting someone else before Jeana auditions.

Option B: Jeana should call her doctor and get two prescriptions. The first is a sedative that is strong enough to knock her out once she boards the plane in Seattle so she isn't even aware that she's flying. When Jeana arrives in New York she knows she'll be very groggy, but that's OK since she will be taking a limo to the hotel. On Friday, she can wake a little earlier and take the second prescription – a moderately strong "upper". If everything works as planned, by the time the 4:00pm audition comes around, she'll have enough energy to perform well. The primary drawback to this idea is that prescriptions don't always work on schedule. The sedative might not relax her enough to abate her flight fright. Worse, come 4:00pm Friday, she runs the risk of still feeling sedated or possibly over-energized, either one preventing her from performing at her best for this one-time-only audition.

Option C: Jeana should call the Producer and explain her fear of flying. With the explanation, she can offer the Producer a choice; if he will agree to reschedule the audition for one week from tomorrow, she will take a few days to drive to New York herself. This option is both affordable and sensible and any reasonable person would understand that waiting a few days is worth it if she's truly the talent that her agent represented her as. If waiting an extra week for the audition is not acceptable, Jenna's other offer to the Producer is to fly him to Seattle and audition tomorrow. She would pay his travel expenses; upgrade him to first class; and offer to audition either Friday or Saturday so he could be back in New York by Sunday evening at the latest. The primary drawback to this idea is that it is more inconvenient for the Producer to see Jeana perform and he wouldn't have the same stage or orchestra elements available in Seattle. Further, other members of the Producer's company would not be able to observe the audition.

Option D: If none of the above - what would you advise?

Gary A. Pokorn

Book X: Success is Failure-Driven

Dedicated to those amazing people who unlike me, face each day "doing alright"; which means so much more.

Like Eric.

I have known Eric for more than 30 years. Over that period Eric's Mom and Dad have shared some of his most joyous occasions; and some of his most upsetting events; and in between these highs and lows Eric would tell you that he has been doing alright. And for Eric, doing alright shows how amazing he truly is.

You see, Eric is the strongest person I know. I'll give you an example. Close your eyes and return to the happiest day of your life – feel how you felt during your most exhilarating moments. OK, now think back to how you felt on your saddest, darkest, most depressed day ever. Just set those mental bookmarks in your mind's eye. There is an unbelievably wide and powerful range of human emotion, yes?

For most of us, we migrate from our highest highs and our lowest lows slowly; with long, "recovery" spans of simply feeling average in between. Unfortunately, Eric is different; his mood swings back and forth, between euphoric highs and debilitating lows in a matter of minutes - multiple times - every hour! Now picture your life with his type of mood swings – as if our other challenges aren't enough to deal with.

Rapid Cycling – that's the technical term for Eric and others who suffer from Bi-Polar Disorder. And Eric lives every day with this unwelcome guest. Medical science is not much help. Bi-Polar Disorder is an affliction of the brain; and very difficult to properly diagnose and treat. Trial and error, mostly. That means people with Bi-Polar Disorder typically wind up dealing with this on their own.

Most can't hold down a steady job. Eric can – and he has consistently been a "go to" person for his company. He is a skilled tradesman; good with customers; dependable; hard working; shows up no matter what; a positive attitude that no job is too tough; that's Eric. Most people with Bi-Polar Disorder can't live independently. Eric does – and if you met him, you would never know the internal turmoil he is living with. He has a pleasant personality; a great smile; a nice sense of humor; knowledgeable of current events; just like the rest of us.

But Eric isn't really like the rest of us. Just getting up and facing the day; every day; takes enormous strength. And he offers no excuses – never has. Eric has earned success and experienced failure. No matter; Eric treats each day anew, the best he possibly can. And when you greet him saying, "Hi. How you doing?" you will almost always hear him say, "I'm doing alright".

If Eric does alright each and every day even though feeling these uncontrollable mood swings – should we do any less?

No, I don't have Bi-Polar Disorder, but it lives next door. And though I don't have it, I can see first-hand the strength Eric has as he lives with it. I'm very proud to say that Eric is my son. And one day I hope to learn the source of his amazing strength so I too can be doing alright.

Gary A. Pokorn

Make sure you don't wind up the richest person in the cemetery. You can't do business from there.

Colonel Harlan Sanders

You already have every characteristic necessary for success.

Zig Ziglar

The highly successful use anxiety and stress to spur them on to achievement.

Tom Hopkins

Success seems to be largely a matter of hanging on after others have let go.

William Feather

Success, real success, in any endeavor demands more from an individual than most people are **willing** to offer- not more than they are **capable** of offering.

James Roche

Failure is an intrinsic step toward success.

Clayton M. Christensen

Most businesses succeed only if others also succeed.

Barry J. Nalebuff

Recently, Business Week ran a story called *Great Ad! What's it for?* That headline pretty much sums up my early opinion of the field. Most ads just don't work, literally.

Jeff Bezos

I once heard someone joke that the road to success is marked with many tempting parking places.

Harvey Mackay

Write out a concise closing statement. It should be compact and pointed enough to be remembered when the rest of the presentation has been forgotten.

Geri McArdle

Success is the ability to move from failure to failure without loss of enthusiasm.

Winston Churchill

The focus of the leader's efforts must be to make sure that each partner in the alliance makes money, particularly in the first few engagements. This money primes the pump for the partnership. Once the pump is running, it will feed itself, and the ringleaders can sit back and reap the profits.

Geoffrey Moore

Give me performance over seniority any day of the week.

Larry Bossidy

The best measurement of anything should be: does it work?

Jack London

I've missed more than 9,000 shots in my career. I've lost almost 300 games. Twenty-six times I've been trusted to take the game-winning shot and missed. I've failed over and over and over again in my life. And that is why I succeed.

Michael Jordan

Success is a journey not a destination.

Unknown

Perhaps the most important result of all education is the ability to make yourself do the thing you have to do, when it ought to be done, whether you like it or not: it is the first lesson that ought to be learned; and however early a man's training begins, it is probably the last lesson that he learns thoroughly.

Thomas Henry Huxley

Credentials are not the same as accomplishments.

Robert Half

Merely do what you'd do if you knew what you were doing.

Price Pritchett

Indeed, the drive for progress is never satisfied with the status quo, even when the status quo is working well.

Jim Collins

Strong chieftains always have strong weaknesses. A king's duty is to make chieftain's strength prevail.

Wess Roberts

Business is cooperation when it comes to creating a pie and competition when it comes to dividing it up.

Barry J. Nalebuff

But it is precisely when emerging markets are small – when they are least attractive to large companies in search of big chunks of new revenue – that entry into them is so critical.

Clayton M. Christensen

Huns learn less from success than they do from failure.

Wess Roberts

Waking is one thing; getting out of bed is quite another.

Anthony Burges

Success without honor is an unseasoned dish; it will satisfy your hunger, but it won't taste good.

Joe Paterno

Success never rests. On your worst days, be good. And on your best days, be great. And on every other day, get better.

Carmen Mariano

Work smarter, and as hard as you can.

Tom Hopkins

Execution is really the critical part of a successful strategy. Getting it done, getting it done right, getting it done better than the next person is far more important than dreaming up new visions of the future.

Price Pritchett

What separates those who achieve from those who do not is in direct proportion to one's ability to ask others for help.

Donald Keough

It's not what we are that holds us back. It's what we think we are not.

Rick Berger

Maybe it is best simply to accept the fact that excellence upsets some people. It always has and always will. Live with it.

Larry Bossidy

Good is the enemy of great. The vast majority of companies never become great, precisely because the vast majority become quite good – and this is their main problem.

Jim Collins

If you try too carefully to plan your life, the danger is that you will succeed – succeed in narrowing your options, closing off avenues of adventure that cannot now be imagined.

Harlan Cleveland

Great spirits have always been subjected to violent attacks from mediocre minds.

Albert Einstein

The caption made no reference to his stature as one of the great industrialists of the twentieth century. It simply read:

"David Packard, 1912-1996, Rancher, etc."

Jim Collins

In prospecting you can always say, "I'm sorry I disturbed you; Goodbye." After all, you've just called them; you haven't ruined their life.

Tom Hopkins

Most often today the difference between a company and its competitor is the ability to execute.

Larry Bossidy

Be fearless and maintain low attachment to the outcome.

Unknown

The closer one gets to the top, the more one finds there is no top.

Nancy Barcus

You can't look at two complementary businesses separately and insist that they each make some *target* rate of return. The only question that really matters is whether you will make more money.

Barry J. Nalebuff

We are not permitted to choose the frame of our destiny. But what we put into it is ours.

Dag Hammarskjold

I wake up every morning determined both to change the world and have one hell of a good time. Sometimes this makes planning the day a little difficult.

E.B. White

I cannot do everything; but I will not let what I cannot do interfere with what I can do.

Edward Everett Hale

Intrepid sailors win wars; intimidated sailors lose them.

Larry Bossidy

Just as we develop our physical muscles through overcoming opposition, such as lifting weights, we develop our character muscles by overcoming challenges and adversity.

Stephen R. Covey

Average sales people like to wing it. Champions like to make money. So they don't wing it – they prepare. Intensively.

Tom Hopkins

Through drive for progress, a highly visionary company displays a powerful mix of self-confidence combined with self-criticism.

Jim Collins

Intentions have no value without results.

Unknown

Do it. Fix it. Try it.

Unknown

The greatest danger for most of us is not that we aim too high and miss the mark, but that our aim is too low and we reach it.

Unknown

"IN" vs. "INTO":

> In means you show up physically. Into means that you are totally absorbed - physically, mentally, and emotionally...
> - Just because you're IN a profession does not necessarily mean that you're a professional.
> - Just because you sell something does not necessarily mean that you're a salesperson.

Bob Gilbert

Don't settle for less than your potential. Remember, average is as close to the bottom as it is to the top.

Abigail Van Buren

A retentive memory may be a good thing, but the ability to forget is the true token of greatness.

Elbert Hubbard

Life is a compromise of what your ego wants to do, what experiences tells you to do, and what your nerves let you do.

Bruce Crampton

We have moved from a world where the big eat the small to a world where the fast eat the slow.

Klaus Schwab

When you set your objectives for the year, you record them in concrete. You can change your plans through the year, but you never change what you measure yourself against.

Jim Collins

Striving for excellence motivates you; striving for perfection is demoralizing.

Harriet Beryl Braiker

Success is ninety percent self-discipline, attitude, and self-image – and only 10 percent job skill.

Tom Hopkins

Lesson 2:

Pay fantastic attention to detail. What details get in the way of our being easy to do business with?

Lesson 6:

Reward, recognize and celebrate. How often does good performance go unrecognized?

Tom Connellan

Power is the ability to do good things for others.

Unknown

Make it comfortable to leave the comfort zone and uncomfortable to stay in it.

M. Scott Peck

Goals are dreams with deadlines.

Diana Scharf-Hunt

High achievers love to be measured … because otherwise they can't prove to themselves that they're achieving.

Robert Noyce

There will always be a conflict between "good" and "good enough."

Henry Martin Leland

Comfort is not the objective in a visionary company. Indeed, visionary companies install powerful mechanisms to create discomfort - to obliterate complacency - and thereby stimulate change and improvement before the external world demands it.

Jim Collins

Do something. If it doesn't work, do something else. No idea is too crazy.

Jim Hightower

Long-term loyalty to companies is eroding. But at the same time, our short-term loyalty can be ferocious, because we are all in a heated battle against the competition.

Robert C. Anderson

Life is difficult. This is a great truth, one of the greatest truths. It is a great truth because once we truly see this truth, we transcend it. Once we know that life is difficult – then life is no longer difficult. Because once it is accepted, the fact that life is difficult no longer matters.

M. Scott Peck

The difference between perseverance and obstinacy is that one often comes from a strong will, and the other comes from a strong won't.

Henry Ward Beecher

I love success. I work smart and hard for what I get, so I deserve it all.

Tom Hopkins

Avoid the ladder against the wrong wall syndrome:

> Meaning, we climb the proverbial ladder of success only to find that it's leaning against the wrong wall.

Stephen R. Covey

Failure is the condiment that gives success its flavor.

Truman Capote

We proposed in general that General Motors should place its cars at the top of each price range and make them of such a quality that they would attract sales from below that price, selling to those customers who might be willing to pay a little more for the additional quality, and attract sales also from above that price, selling to those customers who would see the price advantage in a car of close to the quality of higher-priced competition.

Alfred P. Sloan Jr.

Why should I try to build a great company? I believe that it is no harder to build something great than to build something good. It might be statistically more rare to reach greatness, but it does not require more suffering than perpetuating mediocrity.

Jim Collins

Prospecting is simply this: You get on the phone and call possible buyers until you locate one worth seeing in person. Then you go see that person and arrange for him or her to pay your company money. A portion of that money is paid to you.

Tom Hopkins

The 3 B's of Sales:

Be Brief
Be Bright
Be Gone

Jeff Blauvelt

Talent alone won't make you a success or being in the right place at the right time. The most important question is, "Are you ready"?

Johnny Carson

Someone else's goal is always beyond our reach because it isn't ours.

Tom Hopkins

Poise and process... Your job (as a sales manager) is to remove your judgments and be completely clear (to your sales reps) on your process.

Barry Trailer

Manufacturing excellence results from dedication to daily progress. Making something a little bit better every day.

Robert Hall

A man in a hot air balloon realized he was lost. He reduced altitude and spotted a woman below. He descended a bit more and shouted, "Excuse me, can you help me? I promised a friend I would meet him, but I don't know where I am."

The woman below replied, "You're in a hot air balloon hovering approximately 30 feet above the ground. You're between 40 and 41 degrees north latitude and between 59 and 60 degrees west longitude."

"You must be an engineer", said the balloonist. "I am", replied the woman, "How did you know"?

"Well", answered the balloonist, "everything you told me is, technically correct, but I've no idea what to make of your information, and the fact is I'm still lost. Frankly, you've not been much help at all. If anything, you've delayed my trip."

The woman below responded, "You must be in Management." "I am", replied the balloonist, "but how did you know"?

"Well", said the woman, you don't know where you are or where you're going. You have risen to where you are due to a large quantity of hot air. You made a promise, which you've no idea how to keep, and you expect people beneath you to solve your problems. The fact is you are in exactly the same position you were in before we met, but now, somehow, it's my fault."

Unknown

Your dream is not big enough if it doesn't scare you.

Matthias Schmelz

Book XI: Speak Last; Finish First

Dedicated to …

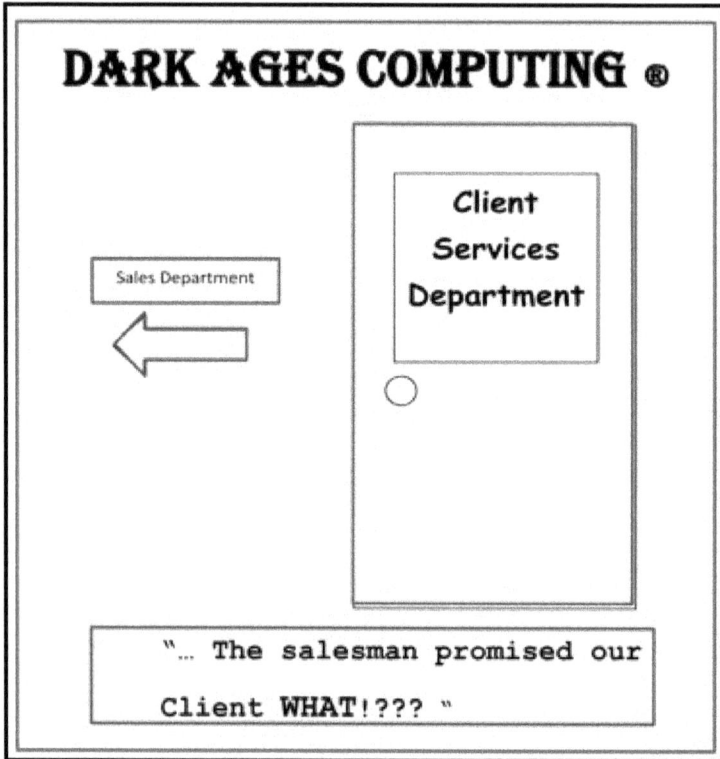

DARK AGES COMPUTING ®

Sales Department

Client Services Department

"… The salesman promised our Client **WHAT**!??? "

Not everyone can do this for a living.

Gary A. Pokorn

Your competition is anyone who raises customer expectations.

Tom Connellan

If you want happy clients, first make sure that your client services employees are happy. Everyone has run into that disgruntled client service representative who hates his job.

Gary A. Pokorn

Training Techniques - Giving Assignments

Hint: People retain and accomplish more when dealing with tasks they are not allowed to complete as opposed to those they are allowed to complete. We are conditioned to complete things. It creates discomfort when we can't, but that discomfort also has a memory value.

Geri McArdle

Give it to me RIGHT.
Give it to me CHEAP.
Give it to me FAST.
Pick Two

Mike King

Getting Started – Focus on Share of Customer, not Market Share.

Seth Godin

Customer relationships are defined by customers.

> Jim Sterne

Treat your own customers better than your rivals' customers.

> Barry Nalebuff

By asking the person to self-assess, before giving the coach's own view, the coach not only gains insight into the person's judgment and knowledge but also can put the responsibility of development on the person.

> Linda Richardson

Say, "Thank You." Create loyalty by rewarding it.

> Barry Nalebuff

Personalized customer service works when you remember that customers want four things:

1. Remember me
2. Communicate with me
3. Work with me
4. Make my life easier.

> Jim Sterne

In every case, the companies who control the customer relationship have the greatest leverage.

Geoffrey Moore

Setting the objective is important. Often when coaches have an objective in mind, it is in the form of what they do not want to see rather than a clear picture of what they expect. Positive objectives that spell out, "I'd like to see…" are certainly more helpful than those that specify what not to do.

Linda Richardson

The most important thing we have that's hard to duplicate is our culture of customer obsession. It pervades everything. Cultures are impossible to copy; either you have them or you don't.

Jeff Bezos

Sometimes things happen so fast in our business that we have to perform a sort of triage… (which is incomplete and bad customer service).

Tom Connellan

Everyone knows that the customer bats last.

David S. Pottruck

Everyone who works here is expected to work toward being the best he can possibly be at the tasks he's accountable for. When he can't do that, he should act like he is until he gets around to it. And if he's unwilling to act like it, he should leave.

Michael E. Gerber

The bottom line is down where it belongs – at the bottom. Far above it in importance are the infinite number of events that produce the profit or loss, especially those that determine how a company approaches all of its constituents.

Paul Hawken

Welcome to Nordstrom... Here, almost in its entirety, is Nordstrom's employee handbook:

We're glad to have you with our Company.

Our number-one goal is to provide outstanding customer service.

Set both your personal and professional goals high.

We have great confidence in your ability to achieve them.

Bob Nelson

Nine Tips on Saying, "Thank You":

1. Say, "Thank You" in kind, not cash.
2. Save the best, "Thank You" for your best customers.
3. Say, "Thank You" in a way that builds your business.
4. Don't say, "Thank You" too quickly, or too slowly.
5. Say you're going to say, "Thank You."
6. Recognize that you may have to compete for loyalty.
7. Allow your competitors to have loyal customers, too.
8. Don't forget to say, "Thank You" even if you have a monopoly.
9. Say, "Thank You" to your suppliers as well as to your customers."

Barry J. Nalebuff

If your customer doesn't perceive he needs something, he doesn't, even if he actually does.

Michael E. Gerber

But even top management types are mostly harmless when you get to know them. Given lots of love, some even make good pets.

Rick Levine

Lesson 5:

Customers are best heard through many ears.

Tom Connellan

The golden rule of feedback – "They speak first."

Linda Richardson

About 30 percent of my clients have had a true Six Sigma cultural transformation; about 50 percent of my clients have obtained tactical results that justified their investment in paying my outrageous fees. And about 20 percent of clients have totally wasted their money.

George Eckes

Get permission from users to maintain an ongoing dialog so you can turn the original attention into a beneficial experience for users and an ongoing profit stream for you.

Seth Godin

The best measure I know is increased shareholder value. And no company is a success financially or otherwise, without satisfied customers.

Louis V. Gerstner, Jr.

I joined the firm about six months ago. I was surprised at the level of detail that had gone into the preparation for my arrival. The secretary had ordered all the supplies I would need – not just paper and pens, but schedule books and a wall calendar… everything.

Bob Nelson

Many companies offer the best deals to new customers. That's backward. You want to treat your best customers the best.

Barry Nalebuff

Plowing altogether new, fertile ground in the field of warranties, and proffering an iron-clad guarantee to each customer: If anything breaks, the customer gets to keep both parts.

Norman Augustine

I live to create value in people's lives and I measure myself by their reactions. I trade in intangibles. I can trade that currency to infinity.

Robert C. Anderson

Common misconceptions about coaching in the marketplace:

- "Coaching is primarily for correcting behavior" - If we only coach people when they do something wrong, we have missed the point. It's about building not fixing.
- "Coaching requires giving up power and control" – the manager relies more on influence. The person is still accountable.
- "Coaching takes too much time" – coaching takes too much time if you don't do enough of it and you don't do it correctly.
- "Coaching is soft stuff" – The manager who avoids soft stuff usually does so because it is so hard. The work is easy; people are difficult.
- "Coaching is laissez-faire management" – Freedom in the workplace, actually just about anywhere, is rooted in strict discipline.
- "Coaching is simply being a good cheerleader" – A good manager has the courage and inner strength when needed to tell people the truth.
- "Coaching is like therapy" – to be a good manager and coach one does need a basic understanding of human behavior and motivation, but therapy has no place in your relationship with the people you are leading.

Unknown

After exhausting every possible way to assist an irate client for the past 45 minutes, and then concluding her phone conversation in the professional manner she had been trained for, the client service representative was heard to let out a pent-up, rhetorical question of frustration, "What does this *customer want me to do about their problem, perform magic"?*

Gary A. Pokorn

"CLIENT FANTASIES"...

My vendor has a capable, available, affordable, fully staffed, Client Services Department - dedicated and committed to servicing my every need and solving all of my problems.

"VENDOR FANTASIES"...

Our Clients won't notice that we don't.

Gary A. Pokorn

There is only one boss. The customer. And he can fire everybody in the company from the chairman on down, simply by spending his money somewhere else.

Sam Walton

How to Manage an Irate Client Call:

"I'm sorry you're so upset. I really feel your pain. No, I don't think we can fix the problem. No, you can't get your money back. Well, I am the supervisor. Let me transfer you to Mr. Dial Tone…"

Unknown

Book XII: True North

Dedicated to... a crisp night in October;

with a slight breeze blowing through bare trees – waiting for the coming winter. Close your eyes. Can you smell remnants of autumn leaves burning?

To winning the homecoming football game. To being carefree. To a Saturday night party at the teenager's house whose parents are away. Can you hear the kids having fun in the kitchen; the basement; and the backyard, all to the beat of the Rolling Stones?

To couches, blue jeans and sweaters. To the floor lamp reflecting on her blond hair making it shimmer with silvery streaks of light. To the nervous small talk of a teenage boy in the presence of a varsity cheerleader. To the patience of the teenage girl sitting on the couch with the captain of the varsity basketball team. Can you remember when you could actually hear your heart throbbing?

To throw pillows, which come in handy when the small talk runs out – what else can a young boy do? And to playful pillow fights; which lead to gentle wrestling and ultimately to that first kiss. Remember how delicate she felt in your arms – the hint of her perfume – the taste of her lips?

To first dates – dinner and a movie. To the movie *Catch 22* and the Oriental Theatre in downtown

Chicago. To dating the prettiest girl in your high school; to falling in love; to asking her father's permission for her hand in marriage. Were you ever so nervous?

To the tears welling up in my eyes even as I write this short introduction. To all those emotions; all the happiness; all those hopes and all those dreams; some fulfilled, some yet to be; and all that I can remember today as if it just happened yesterday – that I will remember everyday, as long as I live. How can someone be so lucky?

To 1970 - and that Saturday night in October in Elmhurst where I kissed Debbie for the very first time. And to the friend's house whose parents were out – to their couch, their floor lamp, to their throw pillows; and to the Rolling Stones music. Can you imagine being so young, so infatuated, and so in love? I still am.

Gary A. Pokorn

Our values are not luxuries, but necessities – not the salt in our bread but the bread itself.

Jimmy Carter

The shift to Humble Self-Reflection:

Arrogance	Humility
I already know ⟶	I don't know
Self-Doubt ⟶	Confidence
Impervious ⟶	Inquisitive
Feedback averse ⟶	Feedback inviting

Unknown

Life is measured by the number of moments that take our breath away.

Unknown

Success is getting what you want; **happiness** is wanting what you get.

Unknown

A recipe for well-being requires a mix of ample optimism to provide hope, a dash of pessimism to prevent complacency, and enough realism to discriminate those things we can control from those we cannot.

David C. Myers

Now and then it's good to pause in our pursuit of happiness and just be happy.

Unknown

More important than the quest for certainty is the quest for clarity.

Francois Gautier

My therapist told me a way to achieve peace was to finish things I started. Today, I finished 2 bags of potato chips, a lemon pie, a fifth of Jack Daniels, and a small box of chocolate candy. I feel better already!

Unknown

Quality of life depends on what happens in the space between stimulus and response.

Stephen R. Covey

Men are especially prone to thinking of quitting as a matter of pride; to them, asking for help is the same as begging. That's why it takes 500,000 sperm cells to fertilize one egg: men are too proud to ask for directions.

Stephen Schiffman

Not what we give, but what we share. For the gift without the giver is bare.

James Russell Lowell

For peace of mind… resign as General Manager of the universe.

Larry Eisenberg

Home, nowadays, is a place where part of the family waits 'til the rest of the family brings the car back.

Earl Wilson

My friends, the less you see of me the better you will like me.

Abraham Lincoln

But performance is more than the *bottom line*. It is also setting an example. And this requires integrity. Limited only to these twin boundaries, business performance and performance as example and mentor, there should be absolute tolerance and indeed the greatest diversity.

Peter F. Drucker

A successful marriage requires falling in love many times, always with the same person.

Mignon McLaughlin

Flattery is telling others exactly what they think of themselves.

Unknown

"Houseless", adj.

Having paid all taxes on household goods.

Ambrose Bierce

We do not inherit the earth from our ancestors – we borrow it from our children.

Native American proverb

As the pressures of life intensify, sometimes the difference between going after a dream and remaining passive is having someone say, "I believe in you!"

Greg Smalley

The Income Tax has made more liars out of the American people than golf has.

Will Rogers

I carry a picture of myself as a child (about six years old) to remind me of two things:

1. To remember to always look at the world as a child does, with wonder and excitement of what I can become.
2. To remember to forgive and love myself just as I would that innocent child in the picture. Too many grown-ups live their lives feeling guilty over mistakes made or lose time blaming themselves for things that could have been. I remember what it is like to be a child and know that in many ways I am not much different from that boy in the picture.

Guy R. Ratti

I've been on a diet for two weeks and all I've lost is two weeks.

Totie Fields

If you haven't got all the things you want, be grateful for the things you don't have that you didn't want.

Unknown

I have a simple philosophy. Fill what's empty. Empty what's full. And scratch where it itches.

Alice Roosevelt Longworth

I'd like you to imagine that you are about to attend one of the most important occasions of your life. It will be held in a room sufficiently large to seat all of your friends, your family, your business associates – anyone and everyone to whom you are important and who is important to you. Can you see it?

The walls are draped with deep golden tapestries. The lighting is subdued, soft, casting a warm glow on the faces of your expectant guests. Their chairs are handsomely upholstered in a golden fabric that matches the tapestries. The golden carpeting is deeply piled. At the front of the room is a dais, and on the dais a large, beautifully decorated table, with candles burning at either end. On the table, in the center, is the object of everyone's attention. A large, shining, ornate box. And in the box is … you! Stiff as the proverbial board.

Michael E. Gerber

You should not confuse your career with your life.

Dave Barry

Question: How can I calculate my body/fat ratio?

Answer: Well, if you have a body, and you have body fat, your ratio is one-to-one. If you have two bodies, your ratio is two-to-one, etc.

Question: I've heard that cardiovascular exercise can prolong life. Is this true?

Answer: How could that be true? Your heart is only good for so many beats, and that's it. Everything wears out eventually, so how could speeding up your heart make you live longer? If you want to live longer – take a nap.

Question: My wife says I should cut down on meat, and eat more fruits and vegetables. What do you say?

Answer: Look, what does a cow eat? Corn. And what's corn? A vegetable. So a steak is nothing more than an efficient mechanism of delivering vegetables to your system.

Question: Is beer bad for you?

Answer: Look, it goes to the earlier point about vegetables. As we all know, scientists divide everything in the world into three categories: animal, mineral, and vegetable. Well, we all know that beer is not an animal, and it's not on the periodic table of elements, so that only leaves one thing, right? My advice: Have a burger and a beer and tell everyone you're on a vegetarian diet.

Unknown

Never measure your generosity by what you give, but rather by what you have left.

Fulton J. Sheen

This is my land. What kind of man would I be if I didn't make it better.

Balian

We exist temporarily through what we take, but we live forever through what we give.

Douglas M. Lawson

Never be afraid of throwing away what you have. If you can throw it away it is not really yours.

R.H. Tawney

Devote to better living the energy that you could spend in criticism.

Imelda Shanklin

A parent can only be as happy as their most unhappy child.

Unknown

I think every human being, Arthur Levitt or the janitor or the waitress or the doctor or the professor, needs and craves validation and positive feedback.

Meg Whitman

Give us serenity to accept what cannot be changed;

Courage to change what should be changed;

And wisdom to distinguish the one from the other.

Reinhold Niebuhr

Often the difference between a successful marriage and a mediocre one consists of leaving three or four things a day unsaid.

>Harlan Miller

Love is not finding someone you can live with; it's finding someone you cannot live without.

>Rafael Ortiz

I have come to realize that anybody can make money; it is much harder to make a difference.

>James P. Owen

A father carries pictures where his money used to be.

>Unknown

About Life:

>Why do we work? We work to make a living. So if we aren't really living, what is all this work for?

>Amy Robertson

"**Character**" is made by what you stand for; "**Reputation**" by what you fall for.

>Robert Quillen

Life is what happens when we've made other plans.

Susan Jeffers

To really enjoy the better things in life, one must first have experienced the things they are better than.

Oscar Homolka

You know *That Look* women get when they want sex? Me neither.

Steve Martin

It's not who you are underneath, but **what you do** that defines you.

Batman

I take full responsibility for my actions, and for my life. My well-being is in the best hands it could possibly be in: my own.

Tom Hopkins

In life, the best way to make your best contribution is to get better at what you're already good at.

Reggie McNeil

The ultimate measure of a man is not where he stands in moments of comfort and convenience, but where he stands at times of challenge and controversy.

Martin Luther King, Jr.

Friendship is a plant we must often water.

German Proverb

You know your children are growing up when they stop asking you where they came from and refuse to tell you where they're going.

Unknown

Use life to provide something that outlasts it.

B.C. Forbes

I believe in getting into hot water; it keeps you clean.

G.K. Chesterton

Freedom is the right to be wrong; not the right to do wrong.

John G. Diefenbaker

Do all the good you can.
  By all the means you can.
    In all the ways you can.
      In all the places you can.
        At all the times you can.
          To all the people you can.
            As long as you can.

John Wesley

How many observe Christ's birthday; how few His precepts. O 'tis easier to keep a Holiday, than Commandments.

Benjamin Franklin

Teaching kids to count is fine, but teaching them what counts is better.

Bob Talbert

Parenthood has two stages:

When your children ask all the questions,
and when they think they know all the answers.

Unknown

Personality is the original personal property.

Norman O. Brown

As small as it may seem, a good deed is always worth doing.

Spark Matsunaga

You can pay too high for a bit of soft living.

Marg Norton

You are 100 percent responsible for 50 percent of any relationship.

Wyatt Webb

When in your entire life were you the most comfortable? In the womb. Now that's security. Your own pool, all the food you could possibly want, and no taxes.

Tom Hopkins

Act as if your success is certain.

Price Pritchett

Doubt whom you will, but never yourself.

Christian Nestell Bovee

Never believe that a few caring people can't change the world. For, indeed, that's all whoever have.

Margaret Mead

You boys remind me of a farmer friend of mine in Illinois, who said he could never understand why the Lord put the curl in a pig's tail. It never seemed to him to be either useful or ornamental, but he reckoned the Almighty knew what he was doing when he put it there.

Abraham Lincoln

My hopes are not always realized, but I always hope.

Ovid

Imagination is stronger than knowledge.
     Dreams are more powerful than facts.
          Hope always triumphs over experience.

Robert Fulghum

Faced with the choice between changing one's mind and proving that there is no reason to do so, almost everybody gets busy on the proof.

John Kenneth Galbraith

"Maturity":

Acting your age instead of your urge.

Unknown

Ignore the ones who say it's too late to start over.

Max Lucado

There are no exceptions to the rule that everybody likes to be the exception to the rule.

Malcolm Forbes

Difference is the beginning of synergy.

Stephen R. Covey

Oh, you hate your job? Why didn't you say so? There's a support group for that. It's called everybody, and they meet at the bar.

Drew Carey

Life is change…
Growth is optional…
Choose wisely.

Karen Kaiser Clark

To acquire knowledge, one must study; but to acquire wisdom, one must observe.

> Marilyn Vos Savant

Top 10 Reasons to Procrastinate:

  1.

> Unknown

Everyone has patience… I learned to use mine.

> Ignacy Padereroski

You can tell whether a man is clever by his answers.

> You can tell whether a man is wise by his questions.

> Naguib Mahfouz

There are no varying degrees of integrity.

> David Cottrell

Wonder, rather than doubt, is the root of knowledge.

> Abraham Heschel

In youth we learn, in age we understand.

Marcie von Ebner-Eschenbach

The truth doesn't hurt unless it ought to.

B.C. Forbes

Procrastination is the art of keeping up with yesterday.

Donald Robert Perry Marquis

Truth is such a rare thing, it is delightful to tell it.

Emily Dickinson

If you are what you do, then when you don't you aren't.

Wayne Dyer

He that never changes his opinions, never corrects his mistakes, and will never be wiser on the morrow than he is today.

Tyron Edwards

Education is learning what you didn't even know you didn't know.

Daniel Joseph Boorstin

Originality consists of trying to be like everybody else - and failing.

Raymond Radiguet

Sometimes the only difference we can make is passing our wisdom on to someone else who will make the bigger difference.

Linda B. Gray

Do not condemn the judgment of another because it differs from your own. You may both be wrong.

Dandemis

Learn from the skillful:

He that teaches himself hath a fool for his master.

Benjamin Franklin

No thought lives in your head rent free.

T. Harv Eker

If you can't be a genius, imitate the daring.

Eudora Welty

It is better to have a permanent income than to be fascinating.

Oscar Wilde

Patience strengthens the spirit,
  sweetens the temper,
   stifles anger,
    extinguishes envy,
     subdues pride,
      bridles the tongue,
       restrains the hand,
        and tramples upon temptation.

George Horne

It's easier to have the vigor of youth when you're old than the wisdom of age when you're young.

Richard J. Needham

An investment in knowledge pays the best dividends.

Benjamin Franklin

Personal growth and increased confidence take place when we are testing the limits of our lives.

Tom Payne

"Look", she said, "this program will be built on the idea that running is fun, racing is fun, improving is fun, and winning is fun. If you're not passionate about what we do here, then go find something else to do."

Jim Collins

In golf and in life, it's the follow-through that makes the difference. Whether or not we follow through on our ideas, our goals, or our intentions is what really makes the difference. If we don't follow through on our ideas, they become only wishes, and wishes, by themselves don't do anything.

Don Essig

How much pain have cost us the evils which have never happened.

Thomas Jefferson

The great secret of successful marriage is to treat all disasters as incidents and none of the incidents as disasters.

Harold Nicholson

Kindness consists in loving people more than they deserve.

Joseph Joubert

Love is a rock against the wind.

Etheridge Knight

Seek those who find your road agreeable, your personality and mind stimulating, your philosophy acceptable, and your experience helpful. Let those who do not, seek their own kind.

Jean-Henri Fabre

You find yourself refreshed by the presence of cheerful people. Why not make an earnest effort to confer that pleasure on others?

Lydia Maria Child

Our deepest fear is not that we are inadequate. Our deepest fear is that we are powerful beyond measure. It is our light, not our darkness, that frightens most of us. We ask ourselves, "Who am I to be brilliant, gorgeous, talented, and fabulous?"

Nelson Mandela

There will come a time when you believe everything is finished. That will be the beginning.

Louis L'Amour

Life moves pretty fast. If you don't stop and look around once in a while, you could miss it.

Ferris Buehler

To one who has faith, no explanation is necessary. To one without faith, no explanation is possible.

Thomas Aquinas

Book XIII: Final Random Thoughts

This chapter is dedicated to the concept of miscellaneous – sometimes in a tidy world we need to be a little less tidy. Not everyone can do this for a living.

Gary A. Pokorn

The art of medicine consists of amusing the patient while nature cures the disease.

Voltaire

Anyone who has ever built a house will understand the only thing that the general contractor ever manages to get out on time are the bills.

Norman R. Augustine

If Patrick Henry thought that taxation without representation was bad, he should see how bad it is with representation.

The Old Farmer's Almanac

Why does everybody stand up and sing, "Take Me Out to the Ballgame", when they're already there?

Larry Anderson

A little boy received a new drum for Christmas. Shortly thereafter, his father came home from work and the mother told him, "I don't think the man upstairs likes to hear Georgie play his new drum, but he's certainly subtle about it." "How do you know"? asked the father. "Well, this afternoon he gave Georgie a knife and asked him if he knew what was inside the drum."

Herbert Prochnow

EVER WONDER...

> Why the sun lightens our hair, but darkens our skin?
>
> Why women can't put on mascara with their mouth closed?
>
> Why don't you ever see the headline, "Psychic Wins Lottery"?
>
> Why is "abbreviated" such a long word?
>
> Why is it that doctors call what they do *practice*?
>
> Why is it that to stop Windows, you click on *Start*?
>
> Why is lemon juice made with artificial flavor, and dishwashing liquid is made with real lemons?
>
> Why is the man who invests all your money called a broker?
>
> Why is the time of day with the slowest traffic called rush hour?
>
> Why isn't there mouse-flavored cat food?

When dog food is new and improved tasting,
who tests it?

Why didn't Noah swat those two mosquitoes?

Why do they sterilize the needle for lethal
injections?

You know that indestructible black box that is
used on airplanes? Why don't they
make the whole plane out of that stuff?

Why don't sheep shrink when it rains?

Why are they called apartments when they
are all stuck together?

If con is the opposite of pro, is Congress the
opposite of progress?

If flying is so safe, why do they call the airport
the terminal?

Unknown

Imagine you are in a sinking rowboat surrounded by
sharks. You have no oars, just a mirror, but can see land
about one mile away. How would you survive?

(Answer: Stop imagining.)

Unknown

Only in America…
can a pizza get to your house faster than
an ambulance.

Only in America…

 are there handicap parking places in front of a
 skating rink.

Only in America…

 do drugstores make the sick walk all the
 way to the back of the store to get their
 prescriptions while healthy people
 can buy cigarettes at the front.

Only in America…

 do people order double cheeseburgers,
 large fries, and a diet coke.

Only in America…

 do banks leave both doors open and then chain
 the pens to the counters.

Only in America…

 do we leave cars worth thousands of dollars
 in the driveway and put our useless junk in the
 garage.

Only in America…

 do we use answering machines to screen
 calls and then have call waiting so we won't miss a
 call from someone we didn't want to talk to in the
 first place.

Only in America…

 do we buy hot dogs in packages of ten and
 buns in packages of eight. (THIS ONE ALWAYS
 BUGGED ME!)

Only in America...
do we use the word "politics" to describe
the process so well: "Poli" in Latin meaning
"many" and "tics" meaning "bloodsucking
creatures."

Only in America...
do they have drive-up ATM machines
with Braille lettering.

Unknown

In case you needed further proof that the human race is
doomed through stupidity, here are some actual label
instructions on consumer goods:

On a Sears hairdryer:
"Do not use while sleeping."
(That's the only time I have to work on
my hair.)

On a bag of Fritos:
"You could be a winner! No purchase
necessary. Details inside."
(The shoplifter special?)

On a bar of Dial soap:
Directions: "Use like regular soap."
(And that would be how?)

On some Swanson frozen dinners:
"Serving suggestion: Defrost."
(But, it's just a suggestion.)

On Tesco's Tiramisu dessert (printed on the bottom):
> "Do not turn upside down."
>> (Well...duh, a bit late, huh?)

On Marks & Spencer Bread Pudding:
> "Product will be hot after heating."
>> (...and you thought?)

On packaging for a Rowenta iron:
> "Do not iron clothes on body."
>> (But wouldn't this save me more time?)

On Booth's Children Cough Medicine:
> "Do not drive a car or operate
> machinery after taking this medication."
>> (We could do a lot to reduce the rate of construction accidents if we could just get those 5-year- olds with head-colds off those forklifts.)

On Nytol Sleep Aid:
> "Warning: May cause drowsiness."
>> (And... I'm taking this because?)

On most brands of Christmas lights:
> "For indoor or outdoor use only."
>> (As opposed to...what?)

On a Japanese food processor:
> "Not to be used for the other use."
>> (Now, somebody out there, help me on this. I'm a bit curious.)

On Sunsbury's peanuts:
"Warning: contains nuts."
(Talk about a news flash)

On an American Airlines packet of nuts:
"Instructions: open packet, eat nuts."
(Step 3: maybe, uh...fly Delta?)

On a child's Superman costume:
"Wearing of this garment does
not enable you to fly."
(I don't blame the company. I blame the
parents for this one.)

On a Swedish chainsaw:
"Do not attempt to stop chain with your
hands."
(Was there a lot of this happening
somewhere?)

Unknown

Book XIV: Gary's Favorite

This chapter is dedicated to you – the reader; and to the great memories that might have come to your mind when you read these quotes and short stories. To a smile I hope you felt on your face, in your mind, and from your heart. And to your ability to face daily stress and all that can be bad in our world with the steadfast peace and tremendous power that can be attained by maintaining a positive attitude.

Everyone may not be able to do this for a living: but each of us has the personal choice and the absolute ability to do this for our life.

Gary A. Pokorn

Thank you Lord. I may never have a lot; but I have always had enough.

Gary A. Pokorn

After Word

Here's to the Bottom Half

During the drive from the meeting to the restaurant, Phil started the conversation. "It's too bad that they won't have anyone available for our intern program until the start of the fall semester at the earliest."

The consultant replied, "I'd like to get the name of that senior he said he was about to meet with to tell him that he won't be graduating next week. He'll have to return for the fall semester if he wants to get his degree. In my mind, he's a prime candidate for a career in sales."

Tosha, the Human Resource Manager accompanying Phil and the consultant on this trip asked, "You mean the young man who just failed one of his finals making him 2 credits short?"

"Exactly" the consultant answered. "He'd be perfect for your sales intern position." He's local; he's probably available; and he's just starting to get a dose of what the real world is going to be like after college" the consultant elaborated. "As they say, sales is what you do when you can't do anything else." (Little did Phil and Tosha know that their consultant was speaking from personal experience.)

Phil quickly rejoined the discussion. "Even if the college didn't have the stipulation that eligible seniors must be in the upper 10% of their class, we certainly wouldn't consider him; the Dean just said he's in the bottom half of his class. And we would <u>never</u> hire someone from the bottom half of their class."

Phil's last statement was made with his usual voice of authority. A young professional probably in his late 20's (maybe early 30's), Phil was the Division Controller for a large, employer services company. Phil had earned his MBA from Virginia Tech University. It's a good bet that he finished his undergraduate and graduate work in the upper percentiles of his class, too. So here he was, living proof of what has been suspected for quite some time about young men with MBA's – seldom right, but never in doubt.

"Well Phil", the consultant replied, "you know I graduated in the bottom half of my class." A hint of a smile was appearing on the consultant's face. Glancing at Phil and Tosha, both riding in the front seat, he listened intently for their reaction.

Ah, the sweet sound of silence. Here was this consultant that Phil's boss, the Business Unit President, had brought in to help implement key aspects of their division's strategic plan. Having succeeded in the operational deployment of several initiatives over the past two years, even Phil was impressed with the consultant's work. Now the college intern program, although not his original idea, was Phil's baby. The Human Resource Manager, Tosha was a graduate of Roanoke College. She was accompanying the meeting today because of her role in supporting this new intern program as well as her knowledge of the local college.

They had invited the consultant to join them not just because of the Business Unit President's suggestion but because he actually had real-world experience in operating a college intern program earlier in his career. (Real world experience? What a concept!)

The level of professional talent in Roanoke, Virginia was quickly becoming a limiting resource as this division pursued a national growth strategy. So, if they couldn't find qualified, experienced, talent locally (and albeit quaint, Roanoke was not a destination spot for a recruit and transfer option); then the next best thing was to recruit them young; train them; and promote from within.

"Phil, that look on your face is worth today's engagement" the consultant mused. "Of course, I'm still going to send you my invoice." Over the past two years Phil, had developed a very nice working relationship with this consultant. Although they often disagreed on minor points, there was a great deal of mutual respect and synergy towards the overall business objectives.

Over lunch, the three of them had a nice chuckle over Phil's facial expression when he discovered that the consultant they had been paying handsomely for the past two years and quite frankly relying on for the successful execution of their strategic plan had graduated in the bottom half of his class. It may not have changed the student's situation, but it probably helped confirm what Division Controllers have suspected for quite some time too – a consultant is just some guy from out of town, with a briefcase.

He had been day-dreaming. For some reason this weekend had brought back that humorous memory from a few year ago as the consultant visited his alma mater, Knox College. Perhaps it was by comparison. Roanoke College is a small, Liberal Arts school with its heritage dating back to Virginia and Civil War South. Knox College, in Galesburg Illinois – the "Land of Lincoln", and a location of one of the famous Lincoln-Douglas debates where Abraham Lincoln began to articulate his (and the North's) opposition to slavery; was a similar, Liberal Arts institution.

It was thirty five years since the consultant had graduated from Knox College. And yes, it's true; he graduated with a solid, C Average; putting him squarely in the bottom half of his class. The flashback to Phil's facial expression during that car ride returned the same smile from then to the consultant's face today.

He had visited the Knox campus many, many times over the years. Recently, he had been returning every year in October to attend the annual Athletic Hall of Fame dinner and induction ceremonies. And every time he had been on campus he always seemed to feel a little different; a little uncomfortable; a little out of place. Knox College is a very prestigious institution attracting top high school students nationally and internationally. The consultant had graduated in the top 10% of his high school class. He had also scored a 28 on his ACT college entrance exam to qualify for an

Illinois State Academic Scholarship. Never the less, each time he has returned to campus those hidden feelings of self-consciousness resurfaced.

One would think that after thirty five years, he'd get over it! The good news is during this trip he seemed to be making some progress. He often tried to understand the origins of why he always felt uneasy, like he didn't really belong. He reflected on the fact that there are many examples of famous people who didn't excel in college. Leonardo DaVinci was fifty six years old when he painted the Mona Lisa; Bill Gates actually dropped out of college to launch Microsoft. The consultant may not be in their class, but he certainly had led a very successful career. Maybe he needed some personal counseling from another consultant. You know – maybe meet with some guy from out of town, who has a briefcase.

During this year's visit to the Knox campus, he found himself paying closer attention to the introductions and acceptance speeches for the 2009 Hall of Fame inductees. He already knew how many Knox alumni were Doctors of This; Lawyers of That; Executive Vice Presidents from prestigious companies such as Caterpillar and Ingersoll Rand. Even one of his Fraternity Brothers was currently the President of the Wm. Wrigley Company. There were college Trustees from his graduating class; authors; research scientists; successful business owners – the works. As he listened to the acceptance speeches he visualized these new Hall of Famers joining the esteemed ranks too.

Periodically he had received various Knox letters and publications acknowledging alumni who had donated $1,000 every year; $10,000 every year; $100,000 for one fund raising initiative; $1 Million for another. He had met some of their sons and daughters too who were now Knox graduates and have moved on to advanced degrees, research professions, and private practices. Yes, Knox College was a prestigious institution indeed.

The consultant's sons? Blue collar all the way. They work as much with their hands as they do with their minds - just like his father, and father-in-law did. Don't get me wrong; those Grandfathers would be proud of these young men almost as much as he was. In fact, over the years he had lived next door to doctors and lawyers, as well as electricians and cowboys. He had often commented to his wife and sons that he was much more comfortable being around the electricians and cowboys. Not many cowboys have a degree from Knox College.

Imagine that. Here he was a graduate in good standing; had led a successful career as a sales professional and leader for several leading American corporations; now working as a management consultant and being paid for his knowledge, experience and guidance; and he felt more at ease with electricians and cowboys than alumni from his college. But this year's trip to Knox was different; it felt much better. It finally started to dawn on him that it was probably a miracle that he actually graduated from Knox College at all –

albeit in the bottom half of his class. He started to realize that very few others faced with his path would have likely faired any better.

To begin with he wasn't a good student. Oh, he had raw talent. I already pointed out his high school success and academic scholarship award. Even so, he never really learned how to study; how to apply himself intellectually. There wasn't much help from the home front either as he would become the first member of his family to earn a college degree; first on his wife's side of the family too. He never appreciated the time commitment and discipline necessary to excel in college. And even if he did, he probably wouldn't have been able to make that type of commitment anyway.

You see, he married his high school sweetheart when he was twenty (she was only nineteen); it was during the winter of his sophomore year. His bride worked fulltime so he could continue his college education. And how many twenty year old newlyweds do you know that want to study every night and every weekend when they can be with their beautiful bride instead? Even if he wanted to commit to the proper study time, their apartment was so cramped it was nearly impossible to remain comfortable and focused for hours at a time. Besides, there was his young and very beautiful wife always near by; looking, well, young and very beautiful! So no, he wasn't a good student as compared to his contemporaries who have since gone on to storied careers.

Socially, he had not made many lifelong friendships with his classmates either. For one thing, he was the only married man in his Fraternity. And as much as his Fraternity Brothers welcomed his wife as an "honorary member", he was the only Brother who didn't live in the fraternity house. Of course, they hoped he would – actually, they hoped his wife would! See what I mean? Too many hours studying.

He had traveled away from campus most weekends during his first three years at Knox (that is, when he wasn't playing basketball). His Mom had been stricken with cancer when he was in the eighth grade. By the time he attended college, she was terminally ill and participating in a revolutionary (i.e. "experimental") cancer treatment program devised by the same type of research scientists his Knox classmates were aspiring to become. Of course, in those days, the nature of this medical research was to load up his Mom's blood with as much medicine as possible and then measure what she could tolerate without dying from the treatment. Doesn't seem very scientific does it? Her "human laboratory", and that of the hundreds and thousands of cancer patients like her, led to the miracle (and tolerable) cancer treatment we all know today as chemotherapy. But, back then they knew it was just experimental (i.e. only a matter of time), so he drove home many weekends to see her vs. hanging out with his classmates and Fraternity Brothers on campus.

After his Mom died in 1974 at the young age of fifty four, the consultant was proud that he gave his Dad a few pleasant weekends that could be remembered for the rest of his Dad's life. His Dad was his biggest basketball fan. While his Mom was alive she was too, but in her mind sports was definitely less important than earning a college degree. She never did see her dream of her sons graduating from college come true - his older brother earned a degree after she died too. At least she saw the both of them get married.

Turning back to his academic performance, I mentioned during college the consultant was also a jock. And jocks, even at an academic oriented institution like Knox College, were expected to participate in practices and of course play in games. Sitting at tonight's dinner, he remembered that he wasn't just any jock. He was a three year starter on the varsity basketball team; the conference scoring champion his sophomore year; named co-captain of the team his senior year; and broke many game, season and career scoring records. Revisiting those accomplishments perked his mood up a lot!

Tonight he realized that Knox College athletics was better off when he finished than it was when he arrived. But then he thought - great. Here he was; an outstanding athlete at an acclaimed academic institution. Not many of those types in his alumni circle. If his former client Phil was with him at tonight's dinner he'd probably have another eye-opening revelation about that management consultant they had hired. Thinking about Phil returned that smile again to the consultant's face.

Oh by the way; and the reason for attending this honorary dinner every October since 2004? That was the year the consultant was inducted into the Knox/Lombard Athletic Hall of Fame for his individual accomplishments. Not bad for a married student, who carried a C average, don't you think? And in 2005 he was inducted a second time along with the entire varsity team from his senior year – as of this writing, thirty five years later, the last team to represent Knox College in the NCAA Division III basketball tournament. We might consider pardoning the boast filling his mind and contributing to his terrific mood. You see, there are a lot of Knox grads who are doctors, lawyers, and successful business executives; not many however who have been inducted into a hall of fame; any hall of fame – twice!

Yes, this year he was starting to lighten up on his self-portrayed, "outsider" feelings. As he continued to review this new-found confidence, he noticed that he had actually spent more time in the library during the past five campus visits than he had during his entire four years as an undergraduate. (By the way, he graduated in four years too; something becoming more of a rarity today, yes?) Out of nowhere he seemed to be developing a new intellectual yearning, like the undergraduates he saw in the library this trip that were young enough to be his sons and daughters. Where was this yearning coming from?

He noticed that he had learned more about subjects such as Abraham Lincoln; the Civil War; and American

History since becoming a career salesman than he did when he had all of those historical resources at his fingertips as a student. Maybe this was a latent "seed of learning" Knox College had planted thirty five years ago.

And he had started to write – perhaps another talent emerging decades after an unnoticed, intellectual "planting"? He was even being sought out for his knowledge of professional, sales process – one of his clients naming him a "doctor in the science of selling". (Perhaps not exactly the same in the eyes of Knox alumni as an actual doctorate degree, but a high compliment just the same.)

The consultant reflected on the fact that he has been happily married for over thirty seven years and still going strong to that same high school sweetheart who sacrificed her college education so he could pursue his. Together they raised their two sons to be the type of gentlemen and hard workers anyone would be proud to claim as their own. They moved west and bought a small ranch to share with their horses – adopted American Mustangs, what else? Occasionally he even had the opportunity to get a little pay-back-chuckle at the expense of an MBA like Phil. Maybe there was something after all to the slogan about the "Knox Experience"?

So as he drove back to Chicago to catch his flight home he offered a little, silent tribute: "Here's to those of us from the bottom half of our graduating class – as it turns out, life is OK for us down here too." Then is mind turned to another thought. Hmmm – maybe a commencement speech in the making. But then reality returned and he said out loud, "Wait a minute. Inviting me to make a commencement speech for Knox College? After graduating from the bottom half of my class? Get real."

Gary A. Pokorn

1st Intermission: Revisited

Your assignment is to place 9 pigs in the 8 pens (below). No pen can have more than 1 pig placed in it; no pig can be left out of the pens. The configuration of the pens cannot be changed. Your design of the pigs is not important.

The pens:

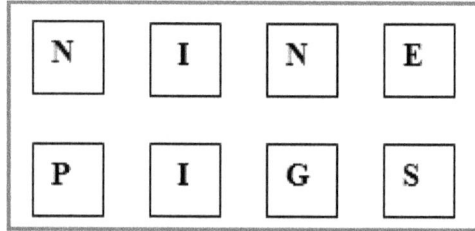

Unknown

April 20, 1999 - Never Forgotten.

We are all Columbine.

www.ingramcontent.com/pod-product-compliance
Lightning Source LLC
Chambersburg PA
CBHW051941090426
42741CB00008B/1220